Now Ready.

Literary Reminiscences and Memoirs of

THOMAS CAMPBELL,

AUTHOR OF "THE PLEASURES OF HOPE."

By his Friend and Coadjutor, CYRUS REDDING,

Author of "Fifty Years' Recollections, Literary and Personal."

"Those in search of a sustained account of Campbell's Life and Works we refer to Mr. Redding's volumes."—*Athæneum*.

"It is with more than ordinary welcome that we receive the present work."—*Leader*.

"The book is a good book....on a highly interesting subject."—*Literary Gazette*.

"Genially and pleasantly written, and giving a very lively insight into the many idiosyncrasies of the poet."—*Critic*.

"Contains a good deal of interesting matter. His history as a poet is well summed up."—*Spectator*.

"Affords an adequate account of the life, both personal and literary, of the poet."—*Illustrated News*.

"Light, racy, and amusing. Full of pleasant gossip about his old friend Campbell."—*West of Scotland Magazine*.

TRAVELS IN MOROCCO,

BY THE LATE

JAMES RICHARDSON,

AUTHOR OF "A MISSION TO CENTRAL AFRICA," "TRAVELS IN THE
DESERT OF SAHARA," &C.

EDITED BY HIS WIDOW.

IN TWO VOLUMES.
VOL. I.

LONDON:
CHARLES J. SKEET, PUBLISHER,
10, KING WILLIAM STREET,
CHARING CROSS.
1860.

LONDON:
Printed by A. Schulze, 13, Poland Street.

INTRODUCTION.

Having made a limited tour in the Empire of Morocco a few years since, I am enabled to appreciate the information imparted to us by the lamented Richardson, and am desirous of adding a few observations of my own upon the present state of affairs in that part of the African Continent.

The following work of the indefatigable traveller demands, at the present moment, a more than ordinary share of public attention, in consequence of the momentous events now passing in the Straits of Gibraltar, where the presence of powerful armaments entails on the Governor of our great rock-fortress, a duty of some delicacy, situated as he now is in close proximity to three belligerent powers, all of whom are at peace with Great Britain. But distinguished alike for common sense and professional ability, Sir William Codrington, it is to be hoped, will steer clear of the follies committed by Sir Robert Wilson in 1844, and will command respect for the British name, without provoking bitter feelings between ourselves, and our French and Spanish neighbours.

It is scarcely possible that either France or Spain can contemplate the conquest of the entire Empire of Morocco, as the result of the present impending crisis, the superficial extent of the territory being 219,420 square miles, and the population nearly 8,000,000,* of which a large proportion live in a state of perpetual warfare, occupying inaccessible mountain fastnesses, from whence they only descend to the plains for the sake of plunder. The inhabitants may be classified as follows : 4,000,000 Moors and Arabs; 2,000,000 Berbers; 500,000 Jews, and the remainder are of the Negro race. The regular Army consists of less than thirty thousand men, but every Arab is an expert irregular horseman, and the Berbers make good footsoldiers.

These indeed are, in ordinary times, rarely to be depended on by the Emperor, but so powerful an incentive is religious fanaticism that, were he to raise the standard of the Holy War, a large Army would quickly rally around him, deficient perhaps in discipline, yet living by plunder, and marching without the encum-

* According to Xavier Darrieu.

brance of baggage, it would prove a formidable opponent.

Let us, however, suppose, that the present action of France and Spain should result in the subversion of the atrocious system of Government practised in Morocco: a guarantee from the conquerors that our existing commercial privileges should be respected, would alone be required to ensure the protection of our interests, and what an extended field would the facilities for penetrating into the interior open to us! We must also remember that Napoleon III. in heart, is a free-trader; and, should Destiny ever appoint him the arbiter of Morocco, the protectionist pressure of a certain deluded class in France would be impotent against his policy in Western Barbary, a country perhaps more hostile to the European than China. Sailors and others, who have had the misfortune to be cast on the inhospitable shore of Northern

Africa, have been sent far inland into slavery to drag out a miserable existence; and, at this moment, there are many white Christian slaves in the southern and eastern provinces of the Empire.

Should the war not result in conquest, the least we have a right to expect, is that toleration should be forced upon the Moors, and that European capital and labour should be allowed a free development throughout their Empire. A flourishing trade would soon spring up, nature having blessed Barbary with an excellent soil and climate, besides vast mineral wealth in its mountains; lead, copper, and antimony are found in them. The plains produce corn, rice, and indigo; the forests of cedar, ilex, cork, and olive-trees are scattered over a vast extent, and contain antelopes, wild bears, and other species of game; Barbary also possesses an excellent breed of horses. The principal manufactures are leather, shawls and carpets.

England has, but a short time since, succeeded in emancipating her Jewish brethren from their few remaining disabilities; an opportunity may now be at hand, of ameliorating the condition of those in the Empire of Morocco, who are forced to submit to a grinding persecution, and are merely tolerated because they are useful. They supply many wants of the Moorish population; are the best, and in many handicrafts, the only artificers, and are much employed by the government in financial occupations. They are compelled to occupy a distinct quarter of the town they inhabit; are permitted only to wear black garments, are forbidden to ride, the horse being considered too noble an animal to carry a Jew, and are forced to take off their shoes on passing a mosque. Even the little Moorish boys strike and ill-treat them in various ways, and the slightest attempt at retaliation was formerly punished with death, and would now be visited with the bastinado. They are more heavily taxed than any other class, and special contributions are often levied on them.

Alas! why should we respect the national existence of any community of Mahometans? Have we effaced from our memory their treachery and inhuman cruelty in India; their utter worthlessness in Turkey; their neglect in taking advantage of the richness with which nature has blest the countries in their possession; and their conquest from Christendom of one of the fairest portions of Europe.

Civilization cries aloud for retribution on a race whose religion teaches them to regard us as "dogs." Surely, far from protecting and cherishing, we should hunt them out of the fair lands they occupy, and force them back on the deserts which vomited them forth on our ancestors ten centuries ago. Brief periods of glory at Bagdad, Cairo, and Granada, should not protect those who are now slaves to the lowest vices that degrade human nature. No administrative reforms are at all practicable; their moral maladies have attacked the vital element; the sole cure is conquest, and the substitution of Christian Governments in Northern Africa, and Turkey in Europe and Asia. Russia, France, Austria, Greece, and Spain are weary of the excesses of their savage neighbours; none can be honestly inclined to stay their avenging swords.

I have, in these prefatory remarks, extracted a few particulars from the short chapter on Morocco, contained in my work on the "French in Africa," and in advocating a crusade against the Mahometan races, I believe I am recording the sentiments of millions of Europeans.

It now only remains for me to give expression to that universal feeling of regret which prevails among my countrymen at the untimely fate of poor Richardson, and to offer my congratulations that he has bequeathed to us so pleasing an addition to his former works as the following narrative of his " Travels in Morocco."

L. TRENT CAVE, F.R.G.S.
Author of " The French in Africa."

Army and Navy Club,
November, 1859.

PREFACE.

THE present unsettled state of affairs in Morocco, in consequence of the War in which she is now engaged with her more powerful and ancient enemy—Spain, must, I conceive, render any information regarding a region so little known peculiarly acceptable at the present moment.

In Morocco, my late husband laboured to advance the same objects which had previously taken him to Central Africa, viz., the amelioration of the condition of the strange and remarkable races of men who inhabit that part of the world. He aimed at the introduction of a legitimate commerce with a view, in the first instance, to destroy the horrible and revolting trade in slaves, and thus pave the way for the diffusion of Christianity among a benighted people. While travelling, with these high purposes in contemplation, he neglected no opportunity of studying the geography of the country, and of obtaining an insight into the manners, customs, prejudices, and sentiments of its inhabitants, as well as any other useful information in relation to it.

I accompanied him on his travels in Algiers, Tunis, and Tripoli, in which last city he left me, it not being considered advisable that I should proceed with him into the interior of the country. We were not destined to meet again in this world. My beloved husband died at Bornou, in Central Africa, whither he was sent by Her Majesty's Governmen to enter into treaties with the chiefs of the surrounding districts.

Of the many difficulties and dangers which the traveller is likely to encounter in penetrating into the interior of so inhospitable a region, the reader may form some idea by a perusal of the the following extracts from my husband's writings.

"I am very much of opinion that in African travel we should take especial care not to attempt too much at once; that we should proceed very slowly, feeling our way, securing ourselves against surprise, and reducing and confining our explorations to the record of matters of fact as far as possible, or consistently with a due illustration of the narrative. But, whether we attempt great tours, or short journeyings, we shall soon find, by our own sad experience, that African travel can only be successfully prosecuted piecemeal, bit by bit, here a little and there a little, now an island, now a line of coast, now an inland province, now a patch of desert, and slow and painful in all their results, whilst few explorers will ever be able to undertake more than two, at most three, inland journeys.

"Failures, disasters, and misadventure may attend our efforts of discovery; the intrepid explorers may perish, as they have so frequently done, or be scalped by the Indian savage in the American wilderness, or stabbed by the treacherous Bedouin of Asiatic deserts, or be stretched stiff in the icy dreary Polar circles, or, succumbing to the burning clime of Africa, leave their bones to bleach upon its arid sandy wastes; yet these victims of enterprise will add more to a nation's glory than its hoarded heaps of gold, or the great gains of its commerce, or even the valour of its arms.

"Nevertheless, geographical discovery is not barren ardour, or wasted enthusiasm; it produces substantial fruits. The fair port of London, with its two parallel forests of masts, bears witness to the rich and untold treasures which result from the traffic of our merchant-fleets with the isles and continents discovered by the genius and enterprise of the maritime or inland explorer. And, finally, we have always in view the complete regeneration of the world, by our laws, our learning, and our religion. If every valley is to be raised, and every mountain laid low, by the spade and axe of industry, guided by science, the valley or the mountain must first be discovered.

"If men are to be civilized, they must first be found; and if other, or the remaining tribes of the inhabitable earth are to acknowledge the true God, and accept His favour as known to us, they also, with ourselves, must have an opportunity of hearing His name pronounced, and His will declared."

My husband would, indeed, have rejoiced had he lived to witness the active steps now taken by Oxford and Cambridge for sending out Missionaries to Central Africa, to spread the light of the Gospel.

Among his unpublished letters, I find one

addressed to the Christian Churches, entitled "Project for the establishment of a Christian Mission at Bornou," dated October, 1849. He writes: "The Christian Churches have left Central Africa now these twelve centuries in the hands of the Mohammedans, who, in different countries, have successfully propagated the false doctrines of the impostor of Mecca. If the Christian Churches wish to vindicate the honour of their religion—to diffuse its beneficent and heavenly doctrines—and to remove from themselves the severe censure of having abandoned Central Africa to the false prophet, I believe there is now an opening, *viâ* Bornou, to attempt the establishment of their faith in the heart of Africa."

He ends his paper by quoting the words of Ignatius Pallme, a Bohemian, the writer of travels in Kordofan, who says "It is high time for the Missionary Societies in Europe to direct their attention to this part of Africa (that is, Kordofan). If they delay much longer, it will be too late; for, when the negroes have once adopted the Koran, no power on earth can induce them to change their opinions. I have heard, through several authentic sources, that there are few provinces in the interior of Africa where Mohammedanism has not already begun to gain a footing."

It would be a great solace to me should this work be received favourably, and be deemed to reflect honour on the memory of my lamented husband; and, in the hope that such may be the case, I venture to commit it into the hands of an indulgent public.

J. E. Richardson.

London,
November 15, 1859.

CONTENTS

OF

THE FIRST VOLUME.

	Page.
Introduction	iii
Preface	xii

CHAPTER I.

Policy of the Court of Morocco.—Its strength.—Diplomatic Intercourse with England.—Distrust of Europeans.—Commercial Relations. 1

CHAPTER II.

Arrival at Tangier.—Moorish Pilgrims in Cordova.—Address of the Anti-Slavery Society.—Mr. D. Hay, British Consul.—Institut d'Afrique.—Conveyance of Eunuchs in vessels under the French Flag.—Franco-Moorish Politics.—Corn Monopolies in Morocco.—Love and veneration for the English name.—Celebration of the Ayd-Kebir, or great festival.—Value of Money in Morocco.—Juvenile Strolling Singer.— General account of the city of Tangier.—Intercourse between the Moorish Emperor and the Foreign Consuls.—Cockney sportsmen.—The degrading of high Moorish Functionaries.—How we smuggle Cattle from Tangier to Gibraltar.—The Blood-letting of plethoric Placemen. 16

CHAPTER III.

The Posada.—Ingles and Benoliel.—Amulets for successful parturition.—Visits of a Moorish Taleb and a Berber.—Three Sundays during a week in Barbary.— M. Rey's account of the Empire of Morocco.—The Government Auctioneer gives an account of Slavery and the Slave Trade in Morocco.—Benoliel as English Cicerone.—Departure from Tangier to Gibraltar.— How I lost my fine green broad-cloth.—Mr. Frenerry's opinion of Maroquine Affairs. 53

CHAPTER IV.

Departure from Gibraltar to Mogador.—The Straits.— Genoese Sailors.—Trade-wind Hurricanes on the Atlantic Coast of Morocco.—Difficulties of entering the Port of Mogador.—Bad provisioning of Foreign Merchantmen.—The present Representative of the once far-famed and dreaded Rovers.—Disembarkation at Mogador.—Mr. Phillips, Captain of the Port.—

CONTENTS. xxiii

Page.

Rumours amongst the People about my Mission.—Visit to the Cemeteries.—Maroquine Wreckers.—Health of the inhabitants of Mogador.—Moorish Cavaliers "playing at powder" composed of the ancient Numidians.—The Barb.—The Life Guards of the Moorish Emperor.—Martial character of the Negro.—Some account of the Black Corps of the Shereefs.—Orthodoxy of the Shereefs, and illustrative anecdotes of the various Emperors. . . . . . . - 81

CHAPTER V.

Several visits from the Moors; their ideas on soldiers and payment of public functionaries.—Mr. Cohen and his opinion on Maroquine affairs.—Phlebotomising of Governors, and Ministerial responsibility.—Border Travels of the Shedma and Hhaha tribes.—How the Emperor enriches himself by the quarrels of his subjects.—Message from the Emperor respecting the Anti-Slavery Address.—Difficulties of travelling through or residing in the Interior.—Use of Knives, and Forks, and Chairs are signs of Social Progress.—Account of the periodical visit of the Mogador Merchants to the Emperor, in the Southern Capital. . 127

CHAPTER VI.

Influence of French Consuls.—Arrival of the Governor of Mogador from the Capital; he brings an order to imprison the late Governor; his character, and mode of administering affairs.—Statue of a Negress at the bottom of a well.—Spanish Renegades.—Various Wedding Festivals of Jews.—Frequent Fêtes and Feastings among the Jewish population of Morocco.—Scripture Illustration, "Behold the Bridegroom cometh!"—Jewish Renegades.—How far women have souls.—Infrequency of Suicides. 176

CHAPTER VII.

Interview with the Governor of Mogador, on the Address of the Anti-Slavery Society.—Day and night side of the Mission Adventure.—Phillips' application to be allowed to stand with his "shoes on" before the Shereefian presence.—Case of the French Israelite, Darmon, who was killed by the Government.—Order of the Government against Europeans smoking in the streets.—Character of Haj Mousa, Governor of Mazagran.—Talmudical of a Sousee Jew.—False weights amongst the Mogador Merchants.—Rumours of war from the North, and levy of troops.—Bragadocio of the Governor.—Mr. Authoris's opinion on the state of of the Country.—Moorish opinions on English Abolition.—European Slavery in Southern Morocco.—Spanish Captives and the London Ironmongers Company.—Sentiments of Barbary Jews on Slavery. . 202

ILLUSTRATIONS.

VOL. I

Interior of a Moorish House.	*Frontispiece.*
City of Tangier.	*Vignette, Title-page.*
Port of Mogador.	89
Christian Burial Place	103
Moorish Cemetery.	105
Nubian Cavalry of Ancient Africa.	111
Wadnoun.	283

VOL. II.

The Snake-Charmer.	*Frontispiece.*
City of Morocco.	*Vignette, Title-page.*
Fish found in Hot Springs.	251
Water-Snake.	252
The Aoudad.	301

TRAVELS IN MOROCCO.

CHAPTER I.

Policy of the Court of Morocco.—Its strength.—Diplomatic Intercourse with England.—Distrust of Europeans.—Commercial Relations.

Morocco is the China of North Africa. The grand political maxim of the Shereefian Court is, the exclusion of strangers; to look upon all strangers with distrust and suspicion; and should they, at any time, attempt to explore the interior of Morocco, or any of the adjacent counties, to thwart and circumvent their enterprise, is a veritable feat of statesmanship in the opinion of the Shereefian Court. The assassination of Mr. Davidson, some years since, is an odious and enduring stigma on the Moorish Court, notwithstanding the various efforts which have been made to deny the personal responsibility of the Emperor in that transaction.

The Prince de Joinville was once going to open Morocco, as we opened China; but bullets and shot which his Royal Highness showered upon Tangier and Mogador, only closed faster the approaches and routes of this well-guarded empire—only more hermetically sealed the capitals of Fez and Morocco against the prying or morbid curiosity of the tourist, or the mappings and measurings of the political spy. The striking anecdote, illustrating the exclusive policy of the Maroquine Court, is familiar to all who have read the history of the Moorish Sultans of the Mugreb. Years ago, a European squadron threatened to bombard Tangier, unless their demands were instantly satisfied; and the then reigning Sultan sent down from Fez this imperial message:

"How much will the enemy give me if I myself burn to ashes my well-beloved city of Tangier? Tell the enemy, O governor of the mighty city of Tangier, that I can reduce this self-same city to a heap of smoking ruins, at a much cheaper rate than he can, with all his ships, his warlike machines, and his fighting men."

The strength of Morocco lies in her internal cities, her inland population, and the natural difficulties of her territory; about her coast she cares little; but the French did not find this out till after their bombardments. The unwonted discovery led them afterwards to boast that they had at length opened Morocco by the other and opposite system of a pacific mission. The parties forming the mission, pretended to have obtained from the Emperor permission for Europeans "to travel in Morocco without let or hindrance whithersoever they will." But the opposition press justly ridiculed the pretensions of the alleged concession, as the precarious and barren result of a mission costing several million of francs. Even an Englishman, but much more a Frenchman—and the latter is especially hated and dreaded in all the Maroquine provinces, would have considerably hesitated in placing confidence in the safe conduct of this jealous Court.

The spirit of the Christian West, which has invaded the most secret councils of the Eastern world, Persia, Turkey, and all the countries subjected to Ottoman rule, is still excluded by the haughty Shereefs of the Mahometan West. There is scarcely any communication between the port and the court of the Shereefs, and the two grand masters of orthodox Islamism, this of the West, and that of the East, are nearly strangers to each other.

All that Muley Errahman has to do with the East, appears to be to procure eunuchs and Abyssinian concubines for his harem from Egypt, and send forward his most faithful, or most rebellious subjects* on their pilgrimage to Mecca.

Englishmen are surprised, that the frequent visits and uninterrupted communications between Morocco and Gibraltar, during so long a period, should have produced scarcely a perceptible change in the minds of the Moors, and that Western Barbary should be a century behind Tunis. This circumstance certainly does not arise from any inherent inaptitude in the Moorish character to entertain friendly relations with Europeans, and can only have re-

---

* It has always been the policy of Mahometan States to send their troublesome subjects, such as were not considered rebel enough to decapitate or to imprison, on a pilgrimage to Mecca. Instead of expiating the sins of a buoyant patriotism at the galleys or the Bermudas, they are sent to slake their patriotic ardour at the holy wells of El-Kaaba.

sulted from that crouching and subservient policy which the Gibraltar authorities have always judged it expedient to show towards the Maroquines.

Our diplomatic intercourse began with Morocco in the reign of Queen Elizabeth; and though on friendly terms more or less ever since, Englishmen have not yet obtained a recognised permission to travel in the interior of the country, without first specially applying to its Government. Our own countrymen know little of Morocco, or of its inhabitants, customs, laws, and government; and, though only five or six days sail from England, it must be regarded as an unknown and unexplored region to the mass of the English nation.

Nevertheless, in spite of the Maroquine Empire being the most conservative and unchangeable of all North African Mussulman states, and whilst, happily for itself, it has been allowed to pursue its course obscurely and noiselessly, without exciting particular attention in Europe, or being involved in the wars and commotions of European nations, Morocco is not, therefore, beyond the reach of changes and the ravages of time, nor exempt from that mutability which is impressed upon all sublunary states. The bombardments of Tangier and Mogador have left behind them traces not easily to be effaced. It was no ordinary event for Morocco to carry on hostilities with an European power.

The battle of Isly has deeply wounded the Shereefians, and incited the Mussulman heart to sullen and unquenchable revenge. A change has come over the Maroquine mind, which, as to its immediate effects, is evidently for the worst towards us Christians. The distrust of all Europeans, which existed before the French hostilities, is now enlarged to hatred, a feeling from which even the English are hardly excepted. Up to the last moment, the government and people of Morocco believed that England would never abandon them to their unscrupulous and ambitious neighbours.

The citizens and merchants of Mogador could not be brought to believe, or even to entertain the idea that the British ships of war would quietly look on, whilst the French—the great rivals and enemies of the English—destroyed their towns and batteries. Most manifest facts and stern realities dissipated, in an hour when they little thought of it, such a fond delusion. From that moment, the moral influence of England, once our boast, and not perhaps unreasonably so, was no longer felt in Morocco; and now we have lost almost all hold on the good wishes and faith of the Mussulman tribes of that immense country.

As to exploring the empire of Morocco, or making it the way of communication with Soudan or Central Negroland, this is now altogether impracticable. The difficulties of Europeans travelling the Maroquine States, always great and perilous, are now become nearly insuperable. This suspicious distrust, or ill-feeling has communicated itself contagiously to the tribes of the South as far as the Desert, and has infected other parts of Barbary. The Engleez, once the cherished friends of the Moors, are looked upon more or less as the abettors of French aggressions in North Africa, if not as the sharers with them of the spoil. In the language of the more plain-spoken Moors, "We always thought all Christians alike, though we often excepted the English from the number of our enemies, now we are certain we were wrong; the English are become as much our enemies as the French and the Spaniards." The future alone can disclose what will be the particular result of this unfavourable feeling; both with respect to France and England, and to other European nations. However, we may look forward without misgiving. Islamism will wear itself out—the Crescent must wane.

In these preliminary observations, the commercial system of the Maroquine Court deserves especial mention. The great object of Muley Abd Errahman* is—nay, the pursuit of his whole life has been—to get the whole of the trade of the empire into his own hands. In fact, he has by this time virtually succeeded, though the thing is less ostentatiously done than by the Egyptian viceroy, that equally celebrated prince-merchant. In order to effect this, his Shereefian Majesty seeks to involve in debt all the merchants, natives, or foreigners, tempting them by the offer of profuse credit. As many of them as are needy and speculative, this imperial boon is without scruple greedily accepted. The Emperor likewise provides them with commodious houses and stores; gives them at once ten or twenty thousand dollars worth of credit, and is content to receive in return monthly instalments. These instalments never are, never can be regularly paid up. The debt progressively and indefinitely increases; and whilst they live like so many merchant-princes, carrying

* The late Emperor of Morocco.

on an immense trade, they are in reality beggars and slaves of the Emperor. They are, however, styled *imperial* merchants, and wear their golden chains with ostentatious pride.

This credit costs his Shereefian Highness nothing; he gives no goods, advances no moneys, whilst he most effectually impoverishes and reduces to servitude the foreign merchant resident in his empire, never allowing him to visit his native country without the guarantee of leaving his wife and family behind as hostages for his return. The native merchant is, in all cases, absolutely at the mercy of his imperial lord. On the bombardment of Mogador, all the native and resident traders, not excepting the English merchants, were found overwhelmed with debt, and, therefore, were not allowed to leave the country; and they were only saved from the pillage and massacre of the ferocious Berber tribes by a miracle of good luck.

Since the bombardment of Mogador, the Emperor has more strongly than ever set his face against the establishment of strangers in his dominions. Now his Imperial Highness is anxious that all commerce should be transacted by his own subjects. The Emperor's Jews are, in future, to be the principal medium of commerce between Morocco and Europe, which, indeed, is facilitated by many of the native Jews having direct relations with European Jews, those of London and Marseilles. In this way, the Maroquines will be relieved from the embarrassments occasioned by the presence of Europeans, Jews, or Christians, under the protection of foreign consuls. The Emperor, also, has a fair share of trade, and gets a good return on what he exports; the balance of commercial transactions is always in his favour.

I must add a word on the way of treating politically with the Court of Morocco. The modes and maxims of this Court, not unlike those of the Chinese, are procrastination, plausible delays, and voluminous despatches and communications, which are carried on through the hands of intermediaries and subordinate agents of every rank and degree. You can never communicate directly with the Emperor, as with other Barbary princes and pashas. This system has admirably and invariably succeeded for the last two or three centuries; that is to say, the empire of Morocco has remained intact by foreign influences, while its system of commerce has been an exclusive native monopoly. The Americans, however, have endeavoured to adopt a more expeditious mode of treating with the Maroquine Court. They have something, in the style and spirit of Lynch law, usually made their own demands and their own terms, by threatening the immediate withdrawal of their consul, or the bombardment of ports.

The Shereefs, thus intimidated, have yielded, though with a very bad grace. Nevertheless, the Americans have received no favours, nor have they obtained a nearer approach to the awful Shereefian presence than other people; and it is not likely they ever will succeed beyond their neighbours. The French and English have always negotiated and corresponded, corresponded and negotiated, and been worsted once and worsted again. Somehow or other, the Emperor has, in most cases, had his own way. Neither the American nor our own European system is the right or dignified course. And I am still of opinion, that the Maroquine Court is so far enlightened respecting the actual state of the barbarians or Christian infidels, out of its Shereefian land of Marabouts, out of its central orthodox Mussulman land of the Mugreb, as to be accessible to ordinary notions of things, and that it would always concede a just demand if it were rightly and vigorously pressed, and if the religious fanaticism of its people were not involved in the transaction. Thus far we may do justice to the government of these Moorish princes.

This opinion, however, does not altogether coincide with that of the late Mr. Hay. According to the report of Mr. Borrow, as found in his work, "The Bible of Spain," the

Moorish government, according to Mr. Hay, was "one of the vilest description, with which it was next to impossible to hold amicable relations, as it invariably acted with bad faith, and set at nought the most solemn treaties." But, if the Maroquine Court had acted in this most extraordinary manner, surely there would now be no Moorish empire of Western Barbary.

CHAPTER II.

Arrival at Tangier.—Moorish Pilgrims in Cordova.—Address of the Anti-Slavery Society.—Mr. D. Hay, British Consul. —Institut d'Afrique.—Conveyance of Eunuchs in vessels under the French Flag.—Franco-Moorish Politics.—Corn Monopolies in Morocco.—Love and veneration for the English name.—Celebration of the Ayd-Kebir, great festival. Value of Money in Morocco.—Juvenile Strolling Singer. —General account of the city of Tangier.—Intercourse between the Moorish Emperor and the Foreign Consuls.— Cockney sportsmen.—The degrading of high Moorish Functionaries.—How we smuggle Cattle from Tangier to Gibraltar.—The Blood-letting of plethoric Placemen.

THE communication between Gibraltar and Tangier is by no means easy and regular, though the places are only a few hours' distance from the other. I had waited many days at Gib. (as our captain called the former place), before the wind enabled us to leave, and then, our boat being a small transport for cattle, and the Government contractors wanting beef for the garrison—for an Englishman or an English soldier cannot live in any part of the world without beef—we were compelled to leave with the wind in our teeth, and to make a night's voyage of this four or five hours' traverse. It might be worth while, one would think, to try a small steam-tug for the conveyance of cattle from Tangier to our garrison, which, besides, would be a great convenience for passengers.

On coming on deck in the morning, Tangier, "the city protected of the Lord," appeared in all its North African lineaments, white and bright, shining, square masses of masonry, domes of fair and modest santos, and the heaven-pointing minarets; here and there a graceful palm, a dark olive, or the black bushy kharoub, and all defined sharply and clearly in the goodly prospect. But these Barbary towns had lost much of their freshness or novelty to me, and novelty is the greatest ingredient of our pleasure in foreign travel. I had also just travelled through Spain, and the south of this country is still, as to its aspect, part and parcel of Morocco, though it is severed by the Straits. In the ancient Moorish city of Cordova, I had even saluted the turban. I met two Moors strolling along, with halting steps and triste mien, through the streets, whom I instinctively addressed.

"*Wein mashe. Ash tomel.* Where are you going? What are you doing?"

The Moors (greatly pleased to hear the sound of their own mother-tongue in the land of their pilgrimage).—"*Net jerrej.* We are enjoying ourselves."

Traveller.—"What do you think of the country (Cordova)?"

The Moors.—"This is the land of our fathers."

Traveller.—"Well, what then? Are you going to possess it again?"

The Moors.—"Of what country are you?"

Traveller.—" Engleez."

The Moors (brightening up).—" That is good. Yes, we are very glad. We thought you might be a Spaniard, or a Frenchman. Now we'll tell you all; we don't fear. God will give us this country again, when Seedna Aïsa* comes to deliver us from these curse-smitten dogs of Spaniards.†"

Traveller.—" Well, never mind the Spaniards. Have you seen anything you like here?"

The Moors.—" Look at this knife; it is rusty; it should not be so."

Traveller.—" How!"

The Moors.—" We read in our books and commentators that in Andalous (Spain) there is no rust, and that nothing rusts here."‡

---

* "Our Lord Jesus," the name by which the Moors always mention Our Saviour.

† Moors entertain the lowest opinion possible of Spaniards. In an intercepted correspondence of the Emperor of Morocco, found at the Battle of Isly, Spaniards are called, "The most degraded of the human race."

‡ The climate of North Africa is remarkable for rusting

Traveller.—"Nonsense; have you seen the hundred pillars of your mosque?" (Now converted into a cathedral.)

The Moors.—"Ah, we have seen them," with a deep sigh; "and the pillars will stand till to-morrow." (End of the world.)

I was obliged to say farewell to these poor pilgrims, wandering in the land of their fathers, and worshipping at the threshold of the noble remains of Moresco-Spanish antiquity, for the *diligencia* was starting off to Seville.

To return from my digression. I soon found myself at home in Tangier amongst my old friends, the Moors, and coming from Spain, could easily recognise many things connecting the one country with the other.

The success attending the various measures of the Bey of Tunis for the abolition of slavery

---

everything which can contract rust. This may be the reason of the Moors representing Spain and other European countries as free from rust, because there it is not so soon contracted.

in North Africa, and the favourable manner in which this prince had received me, when I had charge of a memorial from the inhabitants of Malta, to congratulate his Highness on his great work on philanthropy, induced the Committee of the Anti-Slavery Society to confide to me an address to the Emperor of Morocco, praying him to enfranchise the negro race of his imperial dominions.

We were fully prepared to encounter the strongest opposition from the Shereefian Court; but, at the same time, we thought there could be no insuperable obstacle in our way.

The Maroquines had the same religion and form of government as the Tuniseens, and by perseverance in this, as well as any other enterprise, something might at last be effected. Even the agitation of the question in the empire of Morocco, amongst its various tribes, was a thing not to be neglected; for the agitation of public opinion in a despotic country like Morocco, as well as in a constitutional state like England, admirably prepares the way for great measures of reform and philanthropy; and, besides the business of an abolitionnist is agitation; agitation unceasing; agitation in season and out of season.

On my arrival at Tangier, I called upon Mr. Drummond Hay, the British Consul-General, stating to him my object, and asking his assistance. The English Government had instructed the Consul to address the Emperor on this interesting subject, not long before I arrived, but it was with the greatest difficulty that any sort of answer could be obtained to the communication.

Mr. Hay, therefore, gave me but small encouragement, and was not a little surprised when I told him I expected a letter of introduction from Her Majesty's Government. He could not understand this reiterated assault on the Shereefs for the abolition of slavery, not comprehending the absolute necessity of continued agitation on such a difficult matter, as exciting from a despotic and semi-barbarous prince, fortified by the prejudices of ages and generally sanctioned in his conduct by his religion, the emancipation of a degraded and enslaved portion of the human race.* However, Mr. Hay was polite, and set about arranging matters for proceeding with a confessedly disagreeable subject for any consul to handle under like circumstances. He made a copy of the address of the Anti-Slavery Society, and sent it to the English Government, requesting instructions. I expected an address from the Institut d'Afrique of Paris; but, after waiting some time, the Secretary, Mr.

---

* Lord Palmerston proceeded in the same determined way with the Schah of Persia (See Parliamentary Papers on the Slave Trade, class D, p . ented 1848). But Colonel Shiel was fortunate in obtaining several opinions of Mahomet that —"The worst of men is the seller of men"—was a powerful auxiliary. The perseverance of the Minister and his agents in Persia has been crowned with complete success; the Schah has issued a firman prohibiting the Slave Trade in his territories. This firman will complete our command over the Persian Gulf and the Arabian seas, and enable our cruisers to intercept the slavers from the eastern shore of Africa.

Hippolyte de St. Anthoine, wrote me a letter, in which he stated that, on account of the ill-will manifested by the Emperor to the establishment of the French in Algeria, the Institut had come to the painful conclusion of not addressing him for the abolition of the slave-trade in his imperial states.

Soon after my arrival at Tangier, the English letter-boat, Carreo Ingles, master, Matteo Attalya, brought twelve eunuch slaves, African youths, from Gibraltar. They are a present from the Viceroy of Egypt to the Emperor of Morocco. The Correo is the weekly bearer of letters and despatches to and from Morocco. The slaves were not entered upon the bill of health, thus infringing upon the maritime laws of Gibraltar and Tangier. The other captains of the little boats could not help remarking, "You English make so much fuss about putting down the slave-trade, and allow it to be carried on under your own flag." Even the foreign consuls here reprobated the inconsistency of the British

Government, in aiding the slave-trade of the Mediterranean by their own flag. However, Government ordered a strict inquiry into this case, and took means for preventing the occurrence of a like abuse. Nevertheless, since then the Emperor has actually applied to the British Consul to allow eunuchs to be brought down the Mediterranean in English steamers, in the same way as these were brought from Malta to Gibraltar in the Prometheus—as, forsooth, servants and passengers. And on the refusal of our consul to sanction this illicit conveyance of slaves by British vessels, the Emperor applied to the French consul, who condescended to hoist the tri-coloured flag for the transport of slave-eunuchs! This is one way of mitigating the prejudices of the Shereefian Court against the French occupation of Algeria. Many slaves are carried up and down the Mediterranean in French vessels.

The keeper of an hotel related to me with great bitterness, that the French officer who came with me from Gibraltar had left Tetuan for Algeria. The officer had ordered a great many things of this man, promising to pay on his return to Tangier. He deposited an old hat-box as a security, which, on being opened by the hotel keeper, was found to be full of greasy paper. At Tetuan, the officer gave himself out as a special envoy of the Emperor of the French.

My good friends, the Moors, continue to speculate upon the progress of the French army in Algeria. I asked a Moorish officer what he thought of the rumoured French invasion of Morocco. He put the backs of his hands together, and locking together his fingers to represent the back of a hedgehog, he observed emphatically; "Impossible! No Christians can invade us. Our country is like a hedgehog, no one can touch us." Tangier Christians will never permit the French to invade Morocco, whatever may be the pretext. This is even the opinion of the foreign consuls.

As a specimen of the commercial system of

this country, I may mention that the monopoly of exporting leeches was sold this week to a Jew, at the rate of 25,000 dollars. Now the Jew refuses to buy leeches except at his own price, whilst every unfortunate trader is obliged to sell to him and to him only. In fact, the monopolist fixes the price, and everybody who brings leeches to Tangier must accept it. This case of leeches may be applied to nearly all the monopolies of the country. Can anything be more ruinous to commerce?

All the Moors of Tangier, immediately on entering into conversation with me, inquire if I am Engleez? Even Moorish children ask this question: it appears to be a charm to them. The Ayd Kebir (great feast) was celebrated to day, being the first of the new year. It was ushered in yesterday by prayer in the mosques. About 9 A.M. the governor, the commandant of the troops, and other Tangier authorities, proceeded to the open space of the market, attended with flags and music, and some hundred individuals all dressed in their holiday clothes. The white flag, typical of the sanctity of religion, floated over others of scarlet and green; the music was of squeaking bagpipes, and rude tumtums, struck like minute drums. The greater part were on horseback, the governor being most conspicuous. This troop of individuals ascended a small hill of the market-place, where they remained half an hour in solemn prayer.

No Jew or Christian was allowed to approach the magic or sacred circle which enclosed them. This being concluded, down ran a butcher with a sheep on his back, just slaughtered, and bleeding profusely. A troop of boys followed quickly at his heels pelting him with stones. The butcher ran through the town to the sea-shore, and thence to the house of the Kady—the boys still in hot and breathless pursuit, hard after him, pelting him and the bleeding sheep. The Moors believe, if the man can arrive at the house of the judge before the sheep dies, that the people of Tangier will have good luck; but, if the sheep should be quite dead, and not moving a muscle, then it will bring them bad luck, and the Christians are likely to come and take away their country from them. The drollest part of the ceremony is, that the boys should scamper after the butcher, pelting the sheep, and trying to kill it outright, thus endeavouring to bring ill-luck upon their city and themselves. But how many of us really and knowingly seek our misfortunes? On the occasion of this annual feast, every Moor, or head of a family, kills a sheep. The rich give to the poor, but the poor usually save up their earnings to be able to purchase a sheep to kill on this day. The streets are in different parts covered with blood, making them look like so many slaughter grounds. When the bashaw of the province is in Tangier, thousands of the neighbouring Arabs come to pay him their respects. With the Moors, the festivals of religion are bonâ fide festivals. It may also be added, as characteristic of these North African barbarians, that, whilst many a poor person in our merry Christian England does not, and cannot, get his plum-pudding and roast-beef at Christmas, there is not a poor man or even a slave, in Morocco who does not eat his lamb on this great feast of the Mussulmans. It would be a mortal sin for a rich man to refuse a poor man a mouthful of his lamb.

Of course there was a sensation among the native population, and even among the consular corps, about my mission; but I have nothing very particular to record. I had many Moorish visitors, some of whom were officers of the imperial troops. I made the acquaintance of one, Sidi Ali, with whom I had the following dialogue:—

Traveller.—" Sidi Ali, what can I do to impress Muley Abd Errahman in my favour?"

Sidi Ali.—" Money!"

Traveller.—" But will the Emir of the Shereefs accept of money from us Christians?"

Sidi Ali.—" Money !"

Traveller.—" What am I to give the minister Ben Dris, to get his favour?"

Sidi Ali.—" Money !"

Traveller.—" Can I travel in safety in Morocco?"

Sidi Ali.—" Money :"

Indeed "money" seems to be the all and everything in Morocco, as among us, "the nation of shopkeepers." The Emperor himself sets the example, for he is wholly occupied in amassing treasures in Mequiney. Another acquaintance of mine was a little more communicative.

Aged Moor.—" What can I do for you, stranger? You are good to me, every time I call here you give me tea with plenty of sugar in it. What can I do for you in my country?"

Traveller.—" Tell me how to get on in my mission? How can I see Muley Errahman?"

Aged Moor.—" Now I am bound to give

you my best advice. First then, take plenty of money with you. All love money; therefore without money you can do nothing. Muley Abd Errahman loves money, and money he must have. And the minister loves money, and the minister must not be forgotten. The minister is the door to the Emperor. You cannot get into the house but through the door. Out of the towns and cities, the Emperor has no power; so that whenever you travel out of these places, remember to give the people money."

I had numberless volunteers to conduct me to Fez. All came begging for this honour and lucrative employment. Whatever may be said of the virtues of hospitality, I found all the world alike in its determination to make the most of strangers, if not to devour them. But the Emperor was not at Fez; he was in the southern capital, and it was necessary for me to go viâ Mogador, to endeavour to obtain an interview with him at that place.

The dreary monotony of Moorish life was one day broken in upon by a juvenile strolling singer, who attracted a crowd of silent and attentive listeners. It was a grateful sight to see old men, with long and silvery beards, reclining in mute and serious attention; young men lounging in the pride and consciousness of animal strength; little children intermixed, but without prattle or merriment—all fixed and fascinated with the charm of vocal song. The vocalist himself was a picturesque object; his face was burnt black with Afric's sun, his bare head was wildly covered with long, black matted, and curly hair, but his eye was soft and serene; and, as he stretched his throat upwards to give compass to his voice, he seemed as if he would catch inspiration from the Prophet in heaven. A coarse brown blanket enveloped his spare and way-worn body, his only clothing and shelter from the heat by day and the cold by night, a fold of which fell upon his naked feet.

The voice of the Arab vocalist was extremely plaintive, even to the tones and inflections of distress, and the burden of his song was of religion and of love—two sentiments which all pure minds delight to combine. When he stopped a moment to take breath, a murmur of applause vibrated through the still air of the evening, not indeed for the youth, but for God!* for it was a prayer of the artless and enraptured bystanders, invoking Allah to bless the singing lad, and also to bless them, while ascribing all praise to the Deity.

This devout scene raised the Moors greatly in my estimation. I thought men could not be barbarians, or even a jealous or vindictive race, who were charmed with such simple melody of sounds, and with sentiments so pure and true to nature.

The Arab youth sang:—

* No people understand better than the Moors the noble feeling of gratitude, contained in the words "Non nobis, Domine," &c.

Oh, there's none but the One God!
I'll journey over the Desert far
To seek my love the fairest of maidens;
The camels moan loudly to carry me thither,
Gainly are they, and fleeter than the swift-legged ostrich.
Oh, there's none but the One God!

What though the Desert wind slay me;
What of it? death is from God.
And woe to me! I cannot repine.
But I'll away to the abode of my love,
I'll embrace her with all my strength,
I'll bear her back thence, and rest her on my couch.
Oh, there's none but the One God!

So sang in plaintive accents the youth, until the last ray of the sun lingered on the minarets' tops, when, by the louder and authoritative voice of the Muezin calling the Faithful to prayers, this crowd of the worshippers of song and vocal harmony was dispersed to meet again, and forthwith chant a more solemn strain. The poor lad of the streets and highways went into the mosque along with his motley group of admirers; and all blended their voices and devotion together in prayer and adoration, lowly and in profound prostration, before the Great Allah!

It is my intention, in the course of the present narrative, to give a brief account of the principal towns and cities of North Africa; and I cannot do better than begin with Tangier. This city is very ancient, having probably been built by the aboriginals, Berbers, and was usually called by the Romans, Taigo on Tingis. The Emperor Claudius re-peopled it, and called it Julia Traducta. The Moors call it Sanjah, and relate that Benhad Sahab El-Alem built it, also surrounded it with walls of metal, and constructed its houses of gold and silver. In this condition, it remained until destroyed by some Berber kings, who carried away all its treasures. The modern Tangier is a small city of the province of Hasbat, picturesquely placed on the eastern slope of a hill, which terminates in the west with its port and bay, having some analogy to the site of Algiers. It has almost a square form, and its ramparts are a wall, flanked here and there with towers.

This place, likewise, is most advantageously situate in the narrowest part of the Straits of Gibraltar, at a few miles east of Cape Spartel, and thirty miles W.S.W. of Gibraltar, and has, therefore, been coveted by all the conquerors of North Africa. The Phœnicians, Romans, Goths, and Arabs successively effected its conquest; and it was long a bone of eager contention between the Moors and Portuguese. In 1471, Alonzo, King of Portugal, took it from the Moors; and in 1662 it came into the hands of the English, as a part of the dowry of Catherine, queen of Charles II.; so, whilst in our possession it was a place of considerable strength; but on its evacuation in 1684 by order of the English government, who were disgusted by the expense of its occupation, and the bootless collisions with the natives, the fortifications were demolished, and only the vestiges of them now are visible. Had the British Government continued its occupation for half a century, and kept in check the Maroquine tribes, it is probable that by this time the greater part of Morocco would have been under British rule, when we might have founded a flourishing colony, from which all North Africa might have received the elements of Christian civilization.

Old Tangier (Tangier belia) is situate about four miles east from the present, being now a heap of ruins, near a little river called Khalk or Tingia, spanned over by the remains of a once finely-built Roman bridge. Here was likewise an artificial port, where the Roman galleys retired. The whole of this part of Africa was denominated by the Romans, Mauritania, from the name of this city; and during their administration was united to the government of Spain. Tangier had a population of from four to six thousand. Grabert estimates the population at 10,000, including 2,500 Jews, who live intermixed with the Moors; 1,400 negroes, 300 Berbers of Rif, and about 100 Christians. The Consuls-General of the European Powers reside here; and most of them have commodious houses. The Swedish Consul has a splendid garden, which is thrown open to the European residents. There is but one good street in the town; and the transition from Europe to Barbary, at so short a distance, is striking to the stranger. Tarifa, on the opposite side, along the coast of Spain, has, however, a Moorish affinity to this place; and the dress of the women is not very dissimilar in the two towns, once inhabited by the people of the same religion, and now, perhaps, many of them descendants of the same families.

Tangier, though a miserable place compared to most of the cities in Europe, is something considerable in Morocco, and the great mosque is rather splendid. Mr. Borrow justly remarks that its minarets look like the offspring of the celebrated Giralda of Seville. The Christians have here a convent, and a church within it, to which are attached half-a-dozen monks. There is no Protestant church; Mr. Hay reads service in the British Consulate, and invites the

Protestant residents. Tangier is the only place in the empire where the Christian religion is publicly professed. The Jews have three or four small synagogues. Usually, the synagogues in Barbary are nothing more than private houses.

Before the bombardment of the French, the fortifications mounted forty pieces or so of cannon, but of no strength; on the contrary, going completely to ruin and decay, being scarcely strong enough to fire a salute from. The Bay of Tangier is good and spacious; but, in the course of time, will be filled up with sand. The shipping is exposed to strong westerly winds. The safest anchorage, however, is on the the eastern part, about half a mile off the shore, in a line with the round tower. With a few thousand pounds, one of the finest—at least, one of the most convenient—ports of the Mediterranean could be constructed here. There is a bashaw of this province, who resides at El-Araish, and a lieutenant-governor, who lives at

Tangier. With these functionaries, the representatives of European Powers have principally to transact affairs. On the north is the castle, the residence of the governor.

Eleven consuls take up their abode in Tangier; the British, French, Spanish, Portuguese, American, Danish, Swedish, Sardinian, Neapolitan, Austrian, and Dutch. Each consular house generally belongs to its particular nation, the ground to the Sultan.

The consuls who have the most interest to guard in Morocco, are the British, French, Spanish, and Portuguese. Up to the bombardment of Tangier, the Danish and Swedish Governments paid to the Maroquine Court, the former 25,000 and the latter 20,000 dollars per annum, to have the privilege of hoisting their flag at this port. The French hostilities against Morocco furnished a convenient opportunity for getting this odious tribute abolished. The Americans led the way in getting rid of this subservience to the Shereefian Court, and refused from the first all presents and annual donations. Generally, however, when new consuls are appointed, they bring with them presents, and visit the Emperor in person. On the occasion of *fêtes*, they sometimes make presents to the governors of districts. Whenever the Emperor condescends to come down to Tangier, three days after his arrival, it is the required etiquette for the consuls to seek his presence, and to make their obeisance to the Shereefian Lord. The consuls are accustomed to decide upon and control the affairs of their own countrymen, and those placed under their protection; but when a Moor and an European are concerned in a transaction, it is usually a mixed commission of the consulate and the Moorish authorities.

Many curious anecdotes are current respecting the consuls and the Moorish government. A Spanish consul once took it into his head to strike his flag and leave Tangier. Whilst he was gone, the Emperor ordered all the Jews to go and take possession of his house and live in it, as a degradation. The consular house was soon crammed with dirty Jews, whose vermin and filth rendered the house untenantable, until it had undergone a thorough repair and cleansing. Sometimes the Emperor shows a great affection for a particular consular family. The family of the Portuguese Consul were great favorites. During the war of succession in Portugal, the Portuguese Consul contracted debts in Tangier, not being able to get his salary amidst the strife of parties. The Moors complained to the Emperor of the consul's debts. Muley Abd Errahman, though a thorough miser himself, paid the consul's debts, alleging as a reason, "the consul was a friend of my ancestors, and he shall be my friend." The Portuguese government wished to remove this consul on account of his alleged Miguelite propensities, but the Emperor threatened, if they did, that he would not receive another. Our government compelled the Portuguese to gratify the personal feeling of the Emperor. Senhor Colaso is a native of Morocco, as his father was before him, and the Emperor calls them his own children. The Jewish servants of the consulates are free from the poll-tax and other obnoxious contributions, and their Moorish servants are also exempt from government conscriptions.

At times, very serious misunderstandings and disputes occur between the consuls and the Emperor on the subject of his Imperial Highness. Our consul, Mr. Hay, was shot at by a fanatic marabout, the ball missing him, but killing a horse of one of the party. This affair was passed over, the consul very properly taking no notice of a mad saint. But I will cite another instance, as showing the intimate perception which the Moors have of the peculiar precepts of our religion, as well as exhibiting their own moral ideas, in each case representing them to us in a favourable light. One of the Emperor's subjects had insulted the French consul, M. Sourdeau, and Muley Suleiman addressed to him the following singular epistle.

"In the name of God, the most merciful. There is no power or force except with the Most High and Great God!

"Consul of the French nation, Sourdeau, and salutation to him who is in the right way. Inasmuch as you are our guest, under our protection, and consul in our country of a great nation, so we cannot but wish you the greatest consideration and the honours. On which account, you will perceive that that which has happened to you is to us intolerable, and would still be so had it been done by one of our own children or most intimate friends. And although we cannot put any obstacle to the decrees of God, yet such an act is not grateful to us, even if it is done to the vilest of men, or even cattle, and certainly we will not fail to show an example of severe justice, God willing. If you were not Christians, having a feeling heart, and bearing patiently injuries, after the example of your prophet, whom God has in glory, Jesus the son of Mary, who, in the Book which he brought you in the name of God, commands you, that if any person strike you on one cheek turn to him the other also; and who (always blessed of God!) also did not defend himself when the Jews sought to kill him, from whom God took him. And, in our Book, it is said, by the mouth of our Prophet, there is no people among whom there are so many disposed to good works as those who call themselves Christians; and certainly among you there are many priests and holy men who are not proud; nevertheless, our Prophet also says, that we cannot impute a crime to persons of three sorts, that is to say, madmen (until they return to sound sense), children, and persons who sleep. Now this man who has offended you is mad, and has no knowledge; but we have decreed to give you full satisfaction. If, however, you should be pleased to pardon him, you will perform a magnanimous work, and the Most Merciful will abundantly recompense you. On the other hand, if you absolutely wish him to be punished, he is in your hands, for in my empire no one shall fear injustice or violence, with the assistance of God."

A whimsical story is current in Tangier respecting the dealings of the Shereefian Court with the Neapolitan government, which characteristically sets forth Moorish diplomacy or manœuvring. A ship load of sulphur was sent to the Emperor. The Moorish authorities declared it was very coarse and mixed with dirt. With great alacrity, the Neapolitan government sent another load of finer and better quality. This was delivered; and the Consul asked the Moorish functionaries to allow the coarse sulphur to be conveyed back. These worthies replied, "Oh dear, no! it is of no consequence, the Emperor says, he will keep the bad, and not offend his royal cousin, the King of Naples, by sending it back." The Neapolitan government had no alternative but to submit, and thank the chief of the Shereefs for his extreme condescension in accepting two ship-loads of sulphur instead of one.

There are occasional communications between Tangier and Tarifa, in Spain, but they are very frequent with Gibraltar. A vast quantity of European merchandize is imported here from Gibraltar for Fez and the north of Morocco. All the postal and despatch business also comes through Tangier, which has privileges that few or no other Maroquine cities possess. The emperors, indeed, have been wont to call it "the City of Christians." In the environs, there is at times a good deal of game, and the European residents go out to shoot, as one is wont in other countries to talk a walk. The principal game is the partridge and hare, and the grand sport, the wild boar. Our officers of the Gibraltar garrison come over for shooting. But quackery and humbug exist in everything. A young gentleman has just arrived from Gibraltar, who had been previously six weeks on his passage from Holland to that place, with his legs infixed in a pair of three-league boots. He says he has come from Holland on purpose to sport and hunt in Morocco. Several of the consuls, when they go out sporting, metamorphose themselves into veteran Numidian sportsmen. You would imagine they were going to hunt lions for months in the ravines of the Atlas, whereas it is only to shoot a stray partridge or a limping hare, or perchance they may meet with a boar. And this they do for a couple of days, or twenty-four hours, sleeping during the night very snugly under tents, and fed and feasted with milk, fowls, and sheep by the Arabs.

Morocco, like all despotic countries, furnishes some severe examples of the degrading of high functionaries. There is an old man, Sidi-El-Arby-Es-Said, living there, who is a marked victim of imperial tyranny. Some years ago, the conqueror despoiled him of all his wealth, and threw him into prison, after he had been twenty years bashaw of this district. He was in prison one year with his two sons. The object of the Emperor was to extort the last filse of his money; and he entirely succeeded. The oppressor, however, relented a little on the death of one of his victim's sons; released him from confinement, and gave the ex-bashaw two houses, one for himself and the other for his surviving son. The old captain of the port has been no less than a dozen times in prison, under the exhausting pressure of the Emperor. After the imperial miser has copiously bled his captain, he lets him out to fill his skin again. The old gentleman is always merry and loyal, in spite of the treatment from his imperial taskmaster.

Very funny stories are told by the masters of the small craft, who transport the bullocks from hence to Gibraltar. The government of that place are only allowed to export, at a low duty per annum, a certain number of bullocks. The contractor's agents come over; and at the moment of embarking the cattle, something like the following dialogue frequently ensues.

Agent of Contractor.—" Count away !"

Captain of the Port.—" One, two, three, &c. Thirty, forty. Ah! stop! stop! too many."

Agent of Contractor.—" No, you fool, there are only thirty."

Captain of the Port.—" You lie! there are forty."

Agent of Contractor.—" Only thirty, I tell you," (putting three or four dollars into his hand).

Captain of the Port.—" Well, well, there are only thirty."

And, in this way, the garrison of Gibraltar often gets 500 or 1,000 head of cattle more than the stipulated number, at five dollars per head duty instead of ten. Who derives the benefit of peculation I am unable to state. An anecdote recurs to me of old Youssef, Bashaw of Tripoli, illustrative of the phlebotomizing system now under consideration. Colonel Warrington one day seriously represented to the bashaw how his functionaries robbed him, and took the liberty of mentioning the name of one person. "Yes, yes," observed the bashaw, "I know all about him; I don't want to catch him yet; he's not fat enough. When he has gorged a little more, I'll have his head off."

The Emperor of Morocco, however, usually treats his bashaws of the coast with greater consideration than those of the interior cities, the former being more in contact with Europeans, his Highness not wishing his reputation to suffer in the eyes of Christians.

CHAPTER III.

The Posada.—Ingles and Benoliel.—Amulets for successful parturition.—Visits of a Moorish Taleb and a Berber.—Three Sundays during a week in Barbary.—M. Rey's account of the Empire of Morocco.—The Government Auctioneer gives an account of Slavery and the Slave Trade in Morocco.—Benoliel as English Cicerone.—Departure from Tangier to Gibraltar.—How I lost my fine green broadcloth.—Mr. Frenerry's opinion of Maroquine Affairs.

I TOOK up my stay at the "English Hotel" (posada Ingles), kept by Benoliel, a Morocco Jew, who spoke tolerable English. A Jerusalemitish rabbi came in one day to write charms for his wife, she being near her confinement. The superstition of charms and other cognate matters, are shared alike by all the native inhabitants of Barbary. It often happens that a Marabout shrine will be visited by Moor and Jew, each investing the departed saint with his own peculiar sanctity. So contagious is this species of superstition, that Romish Christians, long resident in Barbary, assisted by the inventive monks, at last discover the Moorish or Jewish to be a Christian saint. The Jewesses brought our Oriental rabbi, declaring him to know everything, and that his garments smelt of the Holy City. Benoliel, or Ben, as the English called him, protested to me that he did not believe in charms; he only allowed the rabbi to write them to please the women. But I have found, during my travels in the Mediterranean, many persons of education, who pretended they did not believe this or that superstition of their church, whilst they were at heart great cowards, having no courage to reject a popular falsehood, and quite as superstitious as those who never doubt the excrescent dogmas or traditionary fables of their religion. The paper amulets, however, operated favourably on Mrs. Benoliel. She was delivered of a fine child; and received the congratulations of her neighbours. The child was named Sultana;* and the people were all as merry as if a princess had been born in Israel.

I received a visit from a Moorish taleb, to whom I read some portions of my journal, as also the Arabic Testament.

Taleb.—" The English read Arabic because they are the friends of Mussulmans. For this reason, God gives them wit to understand the language of the Koran."

Traveller.—" We wish to study all languages, and to know all people."

Taleb.—" Now, as you have become so wise in our country, and read Arabic, where next are

---

* Although *Sultana*, i.e., "Sultanness or Princess," is a frequent name for a woman in this country, I have never heard of a man being called Sultan; and, indeed, I imagine the jealousy of the reigning sovereign would never permit the use of such a name. But even in this country, where women are treated as so many household chattels, Moorish gallantry is sufficient to overlook these trivial or serious pretensions.

you going? Why not be quiet and return home, and live a marabout? Where next are you going?"

In this strain the Taleb continued lecturing me, until he was interrupted by a Berber of Rif.

The Rifian.—" Christian, Engleez, come to our mountains. I will conduct you to the Emir, on whom is the blessing of God. Come to the Emir, come."

Traveller.—" No, I've nothing to do with war."

The Rifian.—" Ah! ah! ah! I know you are a necromancer. Cannot you tell me where money is buried? I want money very bad. Give me a peseta."

Traveller.—" Not I. I am going to see your Emperor."

The Rifian.—" Ah! ah! ah! that is right; give him plenty of money. Muley Abd Errahman hoards up money always. If you give him plenty of money, you will be placed on a horse and ride by his side."

The inhabitants of Barbary all bury their money. The secret is confided to a single person, who often is taken ill, and dies before he can discover the hiding place to his surviving relatives. Millions of dollars are lost in this way. The people, conscious of their secret practice, are always on the scent for concealed treasures.

One Friday, some Jews asked the governor of the custom-house to grant them their clearance-papers, because they were, early on the Sunday following, to depart for Gibraltar. The governor said, "Come to-morrow." "No," replied the Jews, "we cannot, it's our feast." "Well," returned the governor, "you Jews have your feasts, the Christians have theirs, and we Mussulmen will have ours. I'll not go down to the custom-house to day, for it is my feast." These three Sundays or feasts, prevalent through North Africa, are very inconvenient for business, and often make men rebels to their religious persuasions.

The following is a Frenchman's account of Morocco* up to the time of its bombardments.

" The question of Algeria cannot be confined within the limits of the French possessions. It embraces Morocco, a country possessing a vast and varied population. Leo gave a marvellous description of Fez, as the second city of Islamism in his time. Travellers who have sought to explore Africa, rarely or never took the route viâ Morocco. Formerly, monks were stationed in the interior to purchase captives; but, since piracy has ceased, these have left the country. Very few persons go into the interior, for Maroquine merchants come out of their country to trade. Tangier and Tetuan are not fair specimens of Morocco; they form a transition from Europe to Africa, being neither Spain nor Morocco. The ambassador, or merchant, who now-a-days gets an audience with the Sultan, is allowed to see little of the country, arising from

* "Souvenir d'un Voyage du Maroc," par M. Rey, Paris.

the jealousy of the government or native merchants. Davidson was probably murdered by the jealousy of the Fez merchants.

"All the larger cities of Morocco are situate upon the coast, excepting three capitals of the interior—Fez, Miknas, and Morocco, to which El-Kesar-Kebir may be added. The other interior places are mostly large villages, where the tribes of the country collect together. The inhabitants of the cities make gain their only business, and debauchery their only pleasure. As to their learning, there is an immense difference between a Turkish ulema and a Moorish doctor.

"From the fall of Carthage and Rome, until the fourteenth century, the people of North Africa have had relations with Europe. The independence of the kingdoms of Fez and Morocco fell by internal dissensions like the Mussulman power in Spain. After expelling the Mahometans from Spain, the Christians (Spaniards and Portuguese) pursued them to

Morocco, and built a line of forts on its coasts. Those have all now been abandoned except four, held by Spain. England destroyed the fortifications and abandoned Tangier, which she had obtained through Portugal. To blockade Tangier at the present time, would do more harm to England than Morocco, by cutting off the supply of provisions for Gibraltar.

"The navy of Morocco was never very great. It was the audacity and cruelty of its pirates which frightened Christendom. During the maritime wars of the seventeenth and eighteenth centuries, the Emperor of Morocco remained neutral, which was a great benefit to the Christian belligerent powers. Spain must be at peace with Morocco; she must either be an active friend, or an enemy. The policy of Morocco, in former times, was so well managed, that it made all the Christian powers pay a certain tribute to that country, to insure themselves against the piracy of its cruisers.

"The history of the diplomatic relations of Europe with Morocco, presents only a chronicle of shameful concessions made by the European powers to the Moorish princes. At the end of the eighteenth century, the Sultan of Morocco declared that, 'Whoever was not his friend was his enemy,' or, in other words, that 'he would arm his cruisers against every flag which did not float upon a consular house at Tangier.'

"Muley Abd Errahman sent his corsairs to sea in 1828 to frighten the European powers into treaties. The plan succeeded, the first squabble being with Austria. From 1830, or, better to mark the period, since the capture of Algiers, the corsairs and their depredations have ceased. The progress of France in Africa has produced a profound impression in Morocco, but European powers have not taken their due advantage of this. Many humiliating acts have been performed by different governments. England possessed herself of all the commerce of importance since she has been established at Gibraltar. On the whole coast of Morocco, there are only two mercantile establishments under the French flag. French consular agents have no influence with the Moorish government. Morocco and Spain have shewn themselves neighbours. Mutual assistance has often been given by Morocco and Spain, in cases of national distress, particularly in seasons of famine.

"The Sultan of Morocco surveys from a distance the events of Europe, and endeavours to arrest their effect on his frontier. The residence of the foreign consuls was first at Rabat, then at Tangier. The object has constantly been to keep the consuls, as far as possible, from his capital and the transactions of his interior, in order that they may not see the continual revolts of his tribes, and so discover the weakness and disunion of the empire. Communications between Tangier and Morocco require at least forty days, a system shrewdly laid down by the Sultan, who is anxious to be as remote as possible from the consuls and their influence.

"The state of the army and navy, and particularly of the munitions of war, is very bad. All the coast of Morocco is difficult of access, and the only two ports which would have served for a naval station, are those which have been abandoned, viz., the Bay of Santa Cruz and the ancient Mamora, between El-Araish and Rabat; the rest are only roadsteads."

M. Rey thus sums up his observations upon European diplomacy directed towards Morocco. "Voluntary humbling of European nations, always ready to pander to Moorish rapacity, even without reaping any advantage for it; and who submit themselves to be uselessly ransomed. As to the English, they show suppleness and prudence, and sacrificing national dignity to the prosperity of commerce; the Sultans are not backward in taking advantage adroitly of a situation so favourable and almost unique;

such is the picture of the diplomatic relations we have sketched."

He describes the personal character and habits of the Sultan, Muley Abd Errahman, and gives details of the court.

" A Jew is the master-cook of the Emperor, his Imperial Highness always eats alone. The Sultan receives European merchants in a very friendly manner, whilst he keeps ambassadors at a respectful distance. An interview with an ambassador does not last more than ten minutes. The Sultan replies in a phraseology which has not been varied for three centuries. The title of the present vizier is not minister, but sahab, " friend" or " companion." The Sultan has the soundest judgment of any man in his empire, and great tact in the administration of affairs. He instructs himself by continual questions.

" His passion is avarice, and he has converted the whole empire into a commercial firm for the accumulation of his gains. Muley Ismael left a treasury of 100 millions of ducats,* and at the death of Sidi Mohammed, this treasury was reduced to two millions. The constant occupation of Muley Abd Errahman is to replenish the imperial treasury. Commerce, which was neglected by his predecessors, has all his attention. The cruelty of the former sultans is exchanged for the avarice of the present. The history of these Shereefian princes is a chain of unheard-of atrocities. The present sultan keeps not a single promise when his interests interfere."

M. Rey gives us this flattering tableau as a social picture of Morocco.

Covetous governors are continually succeeding one another, they are ever eager of enjoying the advantages of their position; their thirst for plunder is so much the more intense, as they are not allowed time to satisfy it, so they prey on the people. The inhabitants of towns and of the country live in rags in miserable hovels. What

* The value of this ducat is about half-a-crown English money.

raiment! what food! mortality is dreadful, the children are invalids, and the women, especially in the country, are condemned to do the work of beasts of burden ; such is the picture of society.

I have quoted these few passages from the "Mémoire" of M. Rey, because he was resident many years in Tangier, and his account of the country discovers talent and intelligence, but is, of course, coloured with a strong anti-English feeling. Mr. Hay wrote on the back of his Mémoire,—"All that is said in reference to Great Britain is false and malicious." M. Rey's opinions of the Moors and the present governors are still more bitter and unjust.

I had an interview with El-Martel-Warabah, government auctioneer of slaves, from whom I obtained details respecting the slave-trade in Tangier and Morocco generally. There is no market for slaves in Tangier. The poor creatures are led about the town as cattle, particularly in the main street, before the doors of the principal merchants, where they are usually disposed of.

No Jew or Christian is permitted to buy or hold a slave in this country. Government possess many slaves, and people hire them out by the day from the authorities. The ordinary price of a good slave is eighty dollars. Boys, at the age of nine or ten years, sell the best; female slaves do not fetch so much as male slaves, unless of extraordinary beauty. Slaves are imported from all the south.

The Sultan levies no duty on the sale or import of slaves. When one runs away from his master, and takes refuge with another, the new master usually writes to the former, offering to buy him; thus slaves are often enticed away. They are sometimes allowed to abscond without their owners troubling themselves about them, their master's being unable either to feed or sell them.

In cases of punishment for all serious offences, slaves are brought before the judicial authorities, and suffer the same punishment as free men. In cases not deemed grave, they are flogged, or otherwise privately punished by their masters. Slaves went to war with Abd-el-Kader, against the French. The Arabs of Algeria had formerly many slaves. The chief depôt of slaves is Morocco, the southern capital. Ten thousand have been imported during one year; but the average number brought into Morocco is, perhaps, not more than half that amount. The Maroquine Moors, before departing for any country under the British flag, usually give liberty to their slaves. On their return, however, they sell them again as slaves, or get rid of them some way or other. A slave once having tasted of liberty, can never again be fully reconciled to thraldom. Moors resident in Gibraltar, have frequently slaves with them. A few days ago, a slave-boy, resident in Gibraltar, wished to turn Christian, and was immediately sent back to Tangier, and sold to another master.

Europeans, with whom I have conversed in Tangier, assure me that slaves are generally well treated, and that cases of cruelty are rare.

Nevertheless, they eagerly seek their freedom when an opportunity offers. In 1833, a man of great power and influence in the Gharb (province of Morocco), named El-Haj Mohammed Ben El-Arab, on a remonstrance of his slaves, who stated that the English had abolished slavery, and that they ought to have their liberty, called all his slaves together, to the number of seventy-two, and actually took the bold and generous resolution of liberating them. But, before releasing them from bondage, he lectured them upon the difficulty of finding subsistence in their new state of freedom, and then wrote out their *átkas* of liberty. As might have been expected, some returned voluntarily to servitude, not being able to get a living, whilst the greater part obtained an honourable livelihood, enjoying the fruits of independent freedom. It is mentioned, as an instance of fidelity, that a negress is the gaoler of the women in Tangier.*

* Count Grabert gives the following account of Maroquine Blacks: "The Blacks who form a very numerous part of

At every Moorish feast of consequence (four of which are celebrated here in a year), the slaves of Tangier perambulate the streets with music and dancing, dressed in their holiday clothes, to beg alms from all classes of the population, particularly Europeans. The money collected is deposited in the hands of their chief; to this is added the savings of the whole year. In the spring, all is spent in a feast, which lasts seven days. The slaves carry

the population are most of them slaves, and as it is customary in barbarous countries, become an object of trade, though not to be compared with that carried on in other parts of Barbary. The Black is generally of a soft and kind disposition, bears fatigue with patience, and shows a serene and lively temper, totally different in that respect from the Moor, who is taciturn and sullen. Some of them have become men of prosperity and note, after having recovered their liberty. They are renowned for their fidelity, and form the most numerous part of the body-guards of the Sultan; that body-guard makes about the half of the army, which on an average compose a total of ten thousand men. The greater part of those Blacks comes from Senegambia, Guinea, and the dominions of the Fellah or Fellani." (*Specchio geografico e Statistico dell' Impero di Marocco. Geneva.*)

green ears of wheat, barley, and fresh dates about the town. The Moorish women kiss the new corn or fruit, and give the slaves a trifle of money. A slave, when he is dissatisfied with his master, sometimes will ask him to be allowed to go about begging until he gets money enough to buy his freedom. The slave puts the *átka* in his mouth (which piece of written paper when signed, assures his freedom), and goes about the town, crying, " *Fedeeak Allah,* (Ransom of God!)" All depends on his luck. He may be months, or even years, before he accumulates enough to purchase his ransom.

Tangier Moors pretend that the negroes of Timbuctoo sacrifice annually a white man, the victim being preserved and fed for the occasion. When the time of immolation arrives, the white man is adorned with fair flowers, and clothes of silk and many colours, and led out and sacrificed at a grand " fiesta." Slaves and blacks in Morocco keep the same feast, with the difference, that not being able to get a man to sacrifice, they kill a bullock. Such a barbarous rite may possibly be practised in some part of Negroland, but certainly not at Timbuctoo. All these tales about Negro cannibals I am inclined to believe inventions. There never yet has been published a well authenticated case of negro cannibalism.

The grand cicerone for the English at Tangier, is Benoliel. He is a man of about sixty years of age, and initiated into the sublimest mysteries of the consular politics of the Shereefs. Ben is full of anecdotes of everybody and everything, from the emperor on the Shreefian throne, down to the mad and ragged dervish in the streets. Our cicerone keeps a book, in which the names of all his English guests have been from time to time inscribed. His visitors have been principally officers from Gibraltar, who come here for a few days sporting. On the bombardment of Tangier, Ben left the country with other fugitives. The Moorish rabble plundered his house; and many valuables which were there concealed, pledged by persons belonging to Tangier, were carried away. Ben was therefore ruined. Some foolish people at Gibraltar told Ben, that the streets of London were paved with gold, or, at any rate, that, inasmuch as he (Ben) had in his time entertained so many Englishmen at his hospitable establishment at Tangier (for which, however, he was well paid), he would be sure to make his fortune by a visit to England. I afterwards met Ben accidentally in the streets of London, in great distress. Some friends of the Anti-Slavery Society subscribed a small sum for him, and sent him back to his family in Gibraltar. Poor Ben was astonished to find as much misery in the streets of our own metropolis, as in any town of Morocco. Regarding his co-religionists in England, Ben observed with bitterness, "The Jews there are no good; they are very blackguards." He was disappointed at their want of liberality, as well as their want of sympathy for Morocco Jews. Ben thought he knew everything, and the ways of this wicked world, but this visit to England convinced him he must begin the world over again. Our cicerone is very shrewd; withal is blessed with a good share of common sense; is by no means bigoted against Mahometans or Christians, and is one of the more respectable of the Barbary Jews. His information on Morocco, is, however, so mixed up with the marvellous, that only a person well acquainted with North Africa can distinguish the probable from the improbable, or separate the wheat from the chaff. Ben has a large family, like most of the Maroquine Jews; but the great attraction of his family is a most beautiful daughter, with a complexion of jasmine, and locks of the raven; a perfect Rachel in loveliness, proving fully the assertion of Ali Bey, and all other travellers in Morocco, that the fairest women in this country are the Jewesses. Ben is the type of many a Barbary Jew, who, to considerable intelligence, and a few grains of what may be called fair English honesty, unites the ordinarily deteriorated character of men, and especially Jews, born and brought up under oppressive governments. Ben would sell you to the Emperor for a moderate price; and so would the Jewish consular agents of Morocco. A traveller in this country must, therefore, never trust a Maroquine Jew in a matter of vital importance.

Mr. Drummond Hay, our Consul at Tangier, advised me to return to Gibraltar, and to go by sea to Mogador, and thence to Morocco, where the Emperor was then residing. Adopting his advice, I left the same evening for Gibraltar. I took my passage in a very fine cutter, which had formerly been a yacht, and had since been engaged as a smuggler of Spanish goods. I confess, I was not sorry to hear that the Spanish custom-house was often duped. The cutter had been purchased for the Gibraltar secret service.

The Anti-Slavery Society had placed at my disposal a few yards of green cloth, for a present to the minister of the Emperor. At the custom-house of Havre-de-Grace, I paid a heavy duty on it. But, when I got to Irun, on the Spanish frontier, (having determined to come through Spain in order to see the country), the customhouse officers demanded a duty nearly double the cost of the cloth in London, so that there was no alternative but to leave it in their possession. The only satisfaction, or revenge which I had, was that of calling them *ladrones* in the presence of a mob of people, who, to do justice to the Spanish populace, all took my part.

When I complained of this conduct at Madrid, my friends laughed at my simplicity, and told me I was "green" in Spanish; and in travelling through "the land of chivalry," and of "ingeniósos hildágos," ought, on the contrary, to thank God that I had arrived safe at Madrid with a dollar in my pocket; whilst they kindly hinted, if I should really get through the province of Andalusia safe to Cadiz, without being stripped of everything, I must record it in my journal as a miracle of good luck. This was, however, exaggeration. I had no reason to complain of anything else during the time I was in Spain. My fellow travellers (all Spaniards), nevertheless, rebuked me for want of tact. "You ought," they said, "to have given a few pesetas to the guard of the diligencia, who would have taken charge of your cloth, and kept it from going through the custom-house."

On reaching Gibraltar, I made the acquaintance of Frenerry, who for thirty years has been a merchant in Morocco. Mr. Frenerry had frequent opportunities of personal intercourse with Muley Abd Errahman, and had more influence with him than the British Consul. Indeed, at all times, a merchant is always more welcome to his Imperial Highness than a diplomatic agent, who usually is charged with some disagreeable mission. Mr. Frenerry was called, *par excellence*, "the merchant of the West." Of course, Mr. Frenerry's opinions must be

valuable on Maroquine affairs. He says :—
"The Morocco Moors like the English very much, and better than any other Europeans, for they know the English to be their best friends. At the same time, the Moors feel their weakness. They know also, that a day might come when the English would be against them, or have disputes with them, as in days past. The Moors are, therefore, jealous of the English, though they consider them their friends; and do not like Englishmen more than any other Christians to travel in their country. In other respects, if well managed and occasionally coaxed or bribed with a present, the Moors are very good natured, and as tractable as children."

However, I find since the murder of Mr. Davidson, both the people and government of Morocco have got a bad name in Gibraltar; and opinion begins to prevail that it is almost impossible for an Englishman to travel in the country. Mr. Frenerry recommends that a Moor should be treated not proudly, but with a certain degree of firmness, to shew him you will not be trifled with. In this way, he says, you will always continue friends.

With regard to the present Emperor, Mr. Frenerry is a great apologist of his system.

"The Emperor is obliged to exclude foreigners as much as possible from his country. He does not want to tempt the cupidity of Europeans, by showing them the resources of the empire. They are prying about for mines of iron and silver. He is obliged to forbid these geological wanderings. The subjects of his empire are divided in their feelings and interests, and have been driven there by every wave of human revolutions. The Emperor does not wish to discover his weakness abroad, by letting Europeans witness the bad faith and disloyalty of his heterogeneous tribes. The European consuls are much to blame; they always carry their heads too high, if not insolently. They then appoint Jewish consuls along the coast, a class of men whom the hereditary prejudices of his Mussulman subjects will not respect."

There is certainly something, if not a good deal, to be said *for* the emperor as well as *against* him. I was obliged to wait some time at Gibraltar before I could get a vessel for Mogador. I missed one excellent opportunity from the want of a note from the Gibraltar government. A Moor offered to allow me to take a passage without any expense in his vessel, provided I could obtain a note from our government; but the Governor of Gibraltar required an introduction in form, and, before I could receive a letter from Mr. Hay to present to him, the vessel left for Mogador. I therefore lost money and time without any necessity.

CHAPTER IV.

Departure from Gibraltar to Mogador.—The Straits.—Genoese Sailors.—Trade-wind Hurricanes on the Atlantic Coast of Morocco.—Difficulties of entering the Port of Mogador.—Bad provisioning of Foreign Merchantmen.—The present Representative of the once far-famed and dreaded Rovers. — Disembarkation at Mogador.—Mr. Phillips, Captain of the Port.—Rumours amongst the People about my Mission.—Visit to the Cemeteries.—Maroquine Wreckers.—Health of the inhabitants of Mogador.—Moorish Cavaliers "playing at powder" composed of the ancient Numidians.—The Barb.—The Life Guards of the Moorish Emperor.—Martial character of the Negro.—Some account of the Black Corps of the Shereefs.—Orthodoxy of the Shereefs, and illustrative anecdotes of the various Emperors.

On leaving the Straits (commonly called

"The Gut,") a noble sight presented itself—a fleet of some hundred merchantmen, all smacking about before the rising wind, crowding every sail, lest it should change ere they got clear of the obstructive straits. Many weeks had they been detained by the westerly gales, and our vessel amongst the rest. I felt the poignant misery of "waiting for the wind." I know nothing so wearisome when all things are made ready. It is worse than hope deferred, which sickens and saddens the heart.

I have lately seen some newspaper reports, that government is preparing a couple of steam-tugs, to be placed at the mouth of the straits, to tow ships in and out. We may trust it will be done. But if government do it not, I am sure it would answer the purpose of a private company, and I have no doubt such speculation will soon be taken up. Vessels freighted with perishable cargoes are often obliged to wait weeks, nay months, at the mouth of the Straits, to the great injury of commerce. In our days of steam and rapid communication, this cannot be tolerated.*

After a voyage of four days, we found ourselves off the coast of Mogador. The wind had been pretty good, but we had suffered some delay from a south wind, which headed us for a short time. We prayed for a westerly breeze, of which we soon got enough from west and north-west. The first twelve hours it came gently on, but gradually increased till it blew a gale. The captain was suddenly called up in the night, as though the ship was going to sink, or could sink, whilst she was running as fast as we would let her before the wind. But the real danger lay in missing the coast of Mogador, or not being able to get within its port from the violence of the breakers near the shore. Our

---

* Some time since, when the French Government were anxious to get supplies of grain from the Levant, for the north of France, they sent steamers to the Straits, to be ready to tow the vessels through, an example worthy of imitation, in other times besides seasons of famine.

vessel was a small Genoese brig; and, though the Genoese are the best sailors in the Mediterranean—even superior to the Greeks, who rank next—our captain and his crew began to quake. At daylight, the coast-line loomed before us, immersed in fog, and two hours after, the tall minaret of the great mosque of Mogador, shooting erect, a dull lofty pyramid, stood over the thick haze lying on the lower part of the coast.

This phenomenon of the higher objects and mountains being visible over a dense fog on the shore, is frequent on this side of the Atlantic. Wind also prevails here. It scarcely ever rains, but wind the people have nine months out of the twelve. It is a species of trade-wind, which commences at the Straits, or the coasts of Spain and Portugal, and sweeps down northwest with fury, making the entire coast of Morocco a mountain-barrier of breakers, increasing in its course, and extending as far as Wadnoun, Cape Bajdor, Cape Blanco, even to the Senegal.

It does not, however, extend far out at sea, being chiefly confined to the coast range. Our alarm now was lest we should get within the clutches of this fell swoop, for the port once past, it would have required us weeks to bear up again, whilst this wind lasted.

The Atlantic coast of Morocco is an indented or waving line, and there are only two or three ports deserving the name of harbours—harbours of refuge from these storms. Unlike the western coast of Ireland, so finely indented by the Atlantic wave, this portion of the Morocco coast is rounded off by the ocean.

Our excitement was great. The capitano began yelping like a cowardly school-boy, who has been well punched by a lesser and more courageous antagonist. Immediately I got on deck, I produced an English book, which mentioned the port of Mogador as a " good " port.

" Per Dio Santo !" exclaimed our capitano; " yes, for the English it *is* a good port—you dare devils at sea—for them it *is* a good port.

The open sea, with a gale of wind, is a good port for the *maladetti* English."

Irritated at this extreme politeness to our gallant tars, who have so long " braved the battle and the breeze," I did not trouble farther the dauntless Genoese, who certainly was not destined to become a Columbus. Now the men began to snivel and yelp, following the example of their commander. "We won't go into the port, Santa Virgine! We won't go in to be shivered to pieces on the rocks." At this moment our experienced capitano fancied we had got into shoal-water; the surf was seen running in foaming circles, as if in a whirlpool. Now, indeed, our capitano did yelp; now did the crew yelp, invoking all the saints of the Roman calendar, instead of attending to the ship.* Here was a scene of indescribable con-

---

* This conduct of Roman Catholic sailors has often been noticed. Mahometans do the same, and resign themselves to fate, *i.e.*, make no effort to save themselves; the only diffusion. Our ship was suddenly put round and back.

My fellow passengers, a couple of Jews from Gibraltar, began swearing at the capitano and his brave men. One of them, whilst cursing, thought it just as well, at the same time, to call upon Father Abraham. Our little brig pitched her bows two or three times under water like a storm-bird, and did *not* ground. It was seen to be a false alarm. The capitano now took courage on seeing all the flags flying over the fortifications, it being Friday, the Mahometan Sabbath. The silly fellow had heard, that the port authorities always hauled down their colours, when the entrance to the harbour was unsafe by reason of bad weather. Seeing the colours, he imagined all was right.

There are two entrances to the port of Mogador; one from the south, which is quite open; the other from the north-west, which is only a

---

ference is, they are less noisy, and more sullen in their spiritless resignation.

narrow passage, with scarcely room to admit a ship-of-the-line. The 'Suffren,' in which the Prince de Joinville commanded the bombardment of the town, stood right over this entrance, on the northern channel, having south-east the Isle of Mogador, and north-west the coast of the Continent. The Prince took up a bold and critical position, exposed to violent currents, to grounding on a rocky bottom, and to many other serious accidents.*

---

* The entrance to the port of Mogador, however, is difficult to all seamen. We were besides in the depth of winter. The Prince de Joinville describes his mishaps during the height of summer, or in August, when placing his vessels in position before the town. He says in his report of the bombardment: "New difficulties, and of more than one kind awaited us. For four days, the violence of the wind and the roughness of the sea prevented us from communicating with one another. Anchored upon a rocky bottom, our anchors and cables broke, and the loss of them deprived us of resources which were indispensable in order to obtain our object. Some vessels had only one chain and one anchor. We could not think of maintaining ourselves before Mogador under sail. The violence of the currents

As we neared this difficult entrance, we were all in a state of the most feverish excitement,

and of the gale, would probably have carried us too far, and we should have lost the opportunity of acting. Besides, in causing the steamers to get to proceed with us, they would have consumed their fuel, and in leaving them by themselves they would be exposed to run short of provisions and water. It was therefore necessary to remain at anchor. At last, the wind abated, and there remained of the hurricane of the preceding days, a considerable swell from N.N.W. Then the vessels were tormented by the swell, and became ungovernable."

expecting, such was the fury of the breakers, to be thrown on the rock on either side. Thus, it was a veritable Scylla and Charybdis. A man from the rigging descried several small vessels moored snugly behind the isle. We ventured in with breathless agitation. A man from one of the fortifications, guessing or seeing, I suppose, our timidity and bad seamenship, cried out at the top of his lungs, " Salvo !" which being interpreted, meant, " The entrance is safe."

But this was not enough; we were to ha.e another trial of patience. The foolish captain —to terrify us to the last—had to cast his anchor, as a matter of course; and imagine, dear reader, our alarm, our terror, when we heard him scream out, " The chain is snapped !" We were now to be driven out southwards by the fury of the wind, which had become a hurricane, no very agreeable prospect ! Happily, also this was a false alarm. The capitano then came up to me, to shake hands, apologize, and present congratulations on our safe harbouring. The perspiration of fever and a heated brain was coursing down his cheeks. The capitano lit an extra candle before the picture of the Virgin below, and observed to me, whilst the men were saying their prayers of gratitude for deliverance, "Per un miraculo della santissima Vergina; noi sciamo salvati!"—(we are saved by a miracle of the Most Holy Virgin!) which, of course, I did not or could not dispute, allowing, as I do, all men in such circumstances, to indulge freely in their peculiar faith, so long as it does not interfere with me or mine.

It is well that our merchant-vessels have never been reduced to the condition of Genoese craft, or been manned by such chicken-hearted crews. I believe the pusillanimity of the latter is traceable, in a great measure, to the miserable way in which the poor fellows are fed. These Genoese had no meat whilst I was with them. I sailed once in a Neapolitan vessel, a whole month, during which time the crew lived on horse-beans, coarse maccaroni, Sardinian fish, mouldy biscuit, and griping black wine. Meat they had none. How is it possible for men thus fed, to fight and wrestle with the billows and terrors of the deep?

We had no ordinary task to get on shore; the ocean was without, but a sea was within port. The wind increased with such fury, that we abandoned for the day the idea of landing. We had, however, specie on board, which it was necessary forthwith to land. Mr. Philips, captain of the port, and a merchant's clerk, therefore, came alongside with great difficulty in a Moorish boat, to take on shore the specie; and in it I embarked. This said barque was the miserable but apt representation of the by-gone formidable Maroquine navy, which, not many centuries ago, pushed its audacity to such lengths, that the "rovers of Salee" cruised off the English coast, and defied the British fleets. Now the whole naval force of the once-dreaded piratic states of Barbary can hardly boast of two or three badly-manned brigs or frigates. As to

Morocco, the Emperor has not a single captain who can conduct a vessel from Mogador to Gibraltar.

The most skilful *rais* his ports can furnish made an attempt lately, and was blown up and down for months on the coasts of Spain and Portugal, being at last driven into the Straits by almost miraculous interposition.

What was this Moorish boat in which I went on shore? A mere long shell of bad planks, and scarcely more ship-shape than the trunk of a tree hollowed into a canoe, leakily put together. It was filled with dirty, ragged, half-naked sailors, whose seamanship did not extend beyond coming and going from vessels lying in this little port. Each of these Mogadorian port sailors had a bit of straight pole for an oar; the way in which they rowed was equally characteristic. Struggling against wind and current with their Moorish rais at the helm, encouraging their labours by crying out first one thing, then another, as his fancy dictated, the crew repeated in chorus all he said:—"Khobsah!" (a loaf) cried the rais.

All the men echoed "Khobsah."

"A loaf you shall have when you return!" cried the rais.

"A loaf we shall have when we return!" cried the men.

"Pull, pull; God hears and sees you!" cried the rais.

"We pull, we pull; God hears and sees us!" cried the men.

"Sweetmeats, sweetmeats, by G——; sweetmeats by G—— you shall have, only pull away!" swore the rais.

"Sweetmeats we shall have, thank God! sweetmeats we shall have, thank God!" roared the men, all screaming and bawling. In this unique style, after struggling three hours to get three miles over the port, we landed, all of us completely exhausted and drowned in spray.

It is usual for Moors, particularly negroes, to sing certain choruses, and thus encourage one another in their work. What, however, is remarkable, these choruses are mostly on sacred subjects, being frequently the formula of their confession, "There is no God, but one God, and Mahomet is his Prophet," &c. These clownish tars were deeply coloured, and some quite black. I found, in fact, the greatest part of the Moorish population of Mogador coloured persons. We may here easily trace the origin of the epithet " Black-a-Moor," and we are not so surprised that Shakspeare made his Moor black; indeed, the present Emperor, Muley Abd Errahman, is of very dark complexion, though his features are not at all of the negro cast. But he has sons quite black, and with negro features, who, of course, are the children of negresses. One of these, is Governor of Rabat. In no country is the colour of the human skin so little thought of. This is a very important matter in the question of abolition. There is no objection to the skin and features of the negro; it is only the luxury of having slaves, or their usefulness for heavy work, which weighs in the scale against abolition.

As soon as we landed, we visited the lieutenant-governor, who congratulated us on not being carried down to the Canary Islands. Then his Excellency asked, in due studied form:

" Where do you come from ?"

Traveller.—" Gibraltar."

His Excellency.—" Where are you going ?"

Traveller.—" To see the Sultan, Muley Abd Errahman."

His Excellency.—" What's your business ?"

Traveller.—" I will let your Excellency know to-morrow."

I then proceeded to the house of Mr. Phillips, where I took up my quarters. Mr. Willshire, our vice-consul, was absent, having gone up to Morocco with all the principal merchants of Mogador, to pay a visit to the Emperor.

The port of Mogador had to-day a most wild and desolate appearance, which was rendered still more dreary and hideous by a dark tempest sweeping over it. On the shore, there was no appearance of life, much less of trade and shipping. All had abandoned it, save a guard, who lay stretched at the gate of the waterport, like a grim watch-dog. From this place, we proceeded to the merchants' quarter of the town, which was solitary and immersed in profound gloom. Altogether, my first impressions of Mogador were most unfavourable. I went to bed and dreamt of winds and seas, and struggled with tempests the greater part of the night. Then I was shipwrecked off the Canaries; thrown on the coast of Wadnoun, and made a slave by the wild Arabs wandering in the Desert—I awoke.

Mr. Phillips, mine host, soon became my right-hand man. His extraordinary character, and the adventures of his life are worth a brief notice. Phillips said he was descended from those York Jews, who, on refusing to pay a contribution levied on them by one of our most Christian kings, had a tooth drawn out every morning (without the aid of chloroform), until they satisfied the cruel avarice of the tyrant. In person, Phillips was a smart old gentleman, with the ordinary lineaments of his race stamped on his countenance. The greater part of his life has been spent in South America, where he attained the honours of aide-de-camp to Bolivar. In those sanguinary revolutions, heaving with the birth of the young republic, he had often been shut up in the capilla to be shot, and was rescued always by the Jesuit fathers, who pitied and saved the poor Jew, on his expressing himself favourable to Christianity. Returning to England, after twenty years' absence, his mother did not fully recognize him, until he one day got up and admired, with youthful ardour, a china figure on the chimney-piece, which had been his toy in his boyhood. On the occurrence of this little domestic incident, the mother passionately embraced her lost prodigal, once dead, but now "alive again." Phillips came to Mogador on a military speculation, and offered to take the command of the Emperor's cavalry against all his enemies.

This audacity of a Jew filled the Moor with alarm. "How could a Jew, who was not a devil, propose such an insult to the Commander of the Faithful, as to presume to take the charge of his invincible warriors!" Nevertheless, the little fellow weathered the storm, and got appointed "captain of the port of Mogador," with the liberal salary of about thirty shillings per month; but this did not prevent our aide-de-camp, now metamorphosed into a sea captain, from wearing *an admiral's* uniform, which he obtained in a curious way on a visit to England. He met in the streets of London with an acquaintance, who pretended to patronize him. The gentleman jokingly said, "Well, Phillips, I must give you an uniform, since you are appointed captain of the port of Mogador." The said gentleman received, a few months afterwards, when his quondam protégé was safe with his uniform strutting about Mogador, to the amazement of the Moors, and the delight of his co-religionists, a bill of thirty pounds or so, charged for "a suit of admiral's uniform for Mr. Phillips, captain of the port of Mogador;" and found that a joke sometimes has a serious termination.

Phillips, on his first arrival in this country, entered into a diplomatic contest with the Moorish authorities, demanding the privileges of a native British-born Jew, and he determined to ride a horse, in order to vindicate the rights of British Jews, before the awful presence of the Shereefian Court! About this business, the Consul-general Hay is said to have written eleven long, and Mr. Willshire about twenty-one short and pithy despatches, but the affair ended in smoke. Phillips, with great magnanimity and self-denial, consented to relinquish the privilege, on the prayer of his brethren, natives of Mogador, who were very naturally afraid, lest the incensed Emperor might visit on them what he durst not inflict on the British-born Jew.

Of the achievements of Phillips in the way of science (for he assures he is born to the high destiny of enlightening both barbarians and civilized nations) I take the liberty, with his permission, of mentioning one. Phillips brought here a pair of horse-shoes belonging to a dray-horse of the firm of Truman, Hanbury, Buxton, and Co., to astonish the Moors by their size, who are great connoisseurs of horse-flesh. The Moors protested their unbelief, and swore it was a lie,—" such shoes never shod a horse." Phillips then got a skeleton of a head from England. This they also scouted as an imposition, alleging that Phillips had got it purposely made to deceive them. "Although they believed in the Prophet, whom they never saw, they were still not such fools as to believe in everything which an Infidel might bring to their country." Phillips now gave up, in despair, the attempt to propagate science among the Moors.

Our ancient aide-de-camp of Bolivar is a

liberal English Jew, and boasts that, on Christmas-day, he always has his roast-beef and plum-pudding. I supped with him often on a sucking-pig, for the Christians breed pigs in this place, to the horror of pious Mussulmen. This amusing adventurer subsequently left Mogador and went to Lisbon, where he purposed writing a memorial to the Archbishop of Canterbury, containing the plan of a New Unitarian system of religion, by which the Jews might be brought within the pale of the Christian Church!

For some time I felt the effects of my sea voyage; my apartment rocked in my brain. People speculated about the objects of my mission; the most absurd rumours were afloat. "The Christian has come to settle the affairs of Mr. Darman, whom the Emperor killed," some said. Others remarked, "The Christian has come to buy all the slaves of the country, in order to liberate them." The lieutenant-governor sent for Phillips, to know what I came for, who I was, and how I passed my time? Phillips told him all about my mission, and that I was a great taleb. When Phillips mentioned to the governor, that Great Britain had paid a hundred millions of dollars for the liberation of slaves belonging to Englishmen, his Excellency, struck with astonishment, exclaimed, " The English Sultan is inspired by God !"

I visited the burying-place of Christians, situate on the north-side of the town by the

sea-shore. A fine tomb was erected here to the memory of Mrs. Willshire's father. The ignorant country people coming to Mogador stopped to repeat prayers before it, believing it the tomb of some favourite saint. The government, hearing of this idolatry to a Christian, begged Mr. Willshire to have the tomb covered with cement. When this was done, so perverse are these people, that they partially divested it of covering, and chipped off pieces of marble for their women, who ground them into powder, and dusted their faces with it to make them fair. Every six months it is necessary to replaster the tomb. This cemetery is the most desolate place the mind of man can conceive. There is no green turf here to rest lightly on the bosom of the dead! No tree, no cypress of mourning; no shade or shelter for those who seek to indulge in grief. All is a sandy desolation, swept by the wild winds of the solitary shore of the ocean.

Farther on, is the Moorish cemetery, which I passed through. What a spectacle of human corruption! Here, indeed, we may learn to despise this world's poor renown, and cease tormenting ourselves with vain and godless

pursuits. It was then sunset, the moon had risen far up on the fading brow of the departing day, casting pale lights and fearful shadows over this house of the dead. It was time to return, or the gates of the city would shut me out amidst the wreck of poor human dust and bones. I saw, moving in the doubtful shadows of approaching night, the grave-digging hyæna!

It is an ill wind that blows nobody good. The wreckers of this coast boldly assert that a shipwreck is a blessing (*berkah*), sent to them by Providence. The port authorities have even the impudence to declare, that to erect lighthouses at the mouth of the ports would be thwarting the decrees of Divine Providence! In spite of all this, however, at the urgent request of Mr. Willshire, when, on one occasion, the weather was very bad, the governor of Mogador stationed guards on various parts of the coast to preserve the lives and property of shipwrecked vessels. But I do not think I have heard worse cases of Moorish wreckers, than those which have happened not very many years ago on the French and English coasts. Some of my readers will recollect the case of an Indiaman wrecked off the coast of France, when poor ladies in a state of suspended animation, had their fingers cut off to get possession of their diamond-rings. During my stay at Mogador, a courier arrived from Sous, bringing the news of some Christians being wrecked off the coast. A Jew had purchased one poor fellow from the Arabs for two camels. Two others were dead, their bodies cast upon the inhospitable beach by the Atlantic surge, where they lay unburied, to be mangled by the wild tribes, or to feed the hungry hyæna.

Some of the merchants came hither from the capital; amongst the rest, Mr. and Mrs. Elton, they, as well as others, brought a favourable account of the Emperor and his ministers, and lauded very much the commercial policy of the governor of Mogador. Moderation, it is said, is the characteristic of the court's proceedings towards the merchants. Trade was not very brisk, it being the rainy season, when the Arabs are occupied with sowing the ground; the busy time is from September to January.

The produce sold at that time was simply that which is left of the past season, having been kept back with the object of getting a better price for it. Gum is brought in great quantities for exportation. An immense quantity of sugar is imported, a third of which is loaf beet-root sugar brought from Marseilles.

Mr. Phillips came to me, to beg ten thousand pardons for having only fowls for dinner. One morning two bullocks were killed by the Jews, but not " according to the Law," and the greater part of the Jews that day would have to go without meat. On these occasions, the Jews sell their meat to the Moors and Christians at a reduced price. Phillips observed, " I am obliged to eat meat according to the Law, or I should have no peace of my life."

A good many people were affected by colds, but the climate of Mogador is reckoned very good. All the year round there is not much variation; N. W. and N. E. winds bring cold in winter, and cool refreshing breezes in summer. There was not a single medical man in Mogador, although there were some fifty Europeans, including Jews. Some years ago a clever young man was practising here. For one year, each European paid his share of salary; but alas! those whom God blessed with good health, refused to pay their quota to the support of a physician for their sickly neighbours, consequently, every European's life was in the greatest danger, should a serious accident occur to them. With regard to money, they would prefer a broken leg all their life time to paying five pounds to have it set. The consuls of Tangier subscribe for a resident physician.

One afternoon, I went to see the Moorish cavalry "playing at powder," (*Lab Elbaroud*) being a stirring and novel scene. A troop of these haughty cavaliers assembled with their chiefs almost daily on the playa, or parade. Then they divided themselves into parties of twenty or thirty; proceeding with their manœuvres, the cavaliers at first advance slowly in a single line, then canter, and then gallop, spurring on the horse to its last gasp, meantime standing up erect on their shovel-stirrups, and turning from one side to the other; looking round with an air of defiance, they fire off their matchlocks, throw themselves into various dexterous attitudes, sometimes letting fall the bridle. The pieces being discharged, the horses instantaneously stop. The most difficult lesson a barb learns, is to halt suddenly in mid career of a full gallop. To discharge his matchlock, standing on the stirrups while the horse is in full gallop, is the great lesson of perfection of the Maroquine soldiery. The cavaliers now wheel out of the way for the next file, returning reloading, and taking their places to gallop off and fire again. Crowds of people attend these equestrian exhibitions, of which they are passionately fond. They squat round the parade in double or treble rows, muffled up within their bournouses, in mute admiration. Occasionally women are present, but females here join in very few out-door amusements. When a whole troop of cavaliers are thus manœuvering, galloping at the utmost stretch of the horses' muscles, the men screaming and hallowing "hah! hah! hah!" the dust and sand rising in clouds before the foaming fiery barb, with the deafening noise and confusion of a simultaneous discharge of firelocks, the picture represents in vivid colours what might be conceived of the wild Nubian cavalry of ancient Africa.* To-

* The Ancient Numidians rode without saddle or bridle They were celebrated as the "reinless" Numidians—

"Numidæ infraeni."—(Æneid, IV., 41.)

day there was a mishap; several cavaliers did not keep up the line. The chief leading the troops, cried out in a rage, and with the voice of a senator, " Fools! madmen! are you children, or are ye men?" Christians or Jews standing too near, are frequently pushed back with violence; and we were told " not to stand in the way of Mussulmen."

These cavaliers are sometimes called *spahis;* they are composed of Moors, Arabs, Berbers,

---

We are aware that another meaning to *infraeni* has been given, that of "indomitable;" but the peculiarity of these horsemen riding without reins is the usual rendering. But ordinarily, the modern Moorish cavalry is very comfortably mounted. Their saddles, with high backs, are as commodious as a chair. The large, broad, shovel-stirrups enable the rider to stand upright as on terra firma, whilst the sharp iron edges of the stirrups goring the ribs of the poor animal, serve as spurs. These lacerating stirrups are tied up short to the saddle, and the knees of the rider are bent forwards in a very ungainly manner. Nevertheless, the barb delights in the "powder play" as much as his master, and—

"Each generous steed to meet the play aspires,
And seconds, with his own, his master's fires;
He neighs, he foams, he paws the ground beneath,
And smoke and flame his swelling nostrils breathe."

and all the native races in Morocco. They are usually plainly dressed, but, beneath the bournouse, many of them wear the Moorish dress, embroidered in the richest style. Some of the horses are magnificently caparisoned in superb harness, worked in silk and gold. Fine harness is one of the luxuries of North Africa, and is still much used, even in Tunis and Tripoli, where the new system of European military dress and tactics has been introduced. The horse is the sacred animal of Morocco, as well as the safeguard of the empire. The Sultan has no other military defence, except the natural difficulties of the country, or the hatred of his people to strangers. He does not permit the exportation of horses, nor of barley, on which they are often fed.*

* The fire of the Barbary horse is generally known, but few reflect upon the power of endurance which this animal possesses. I have known them to go without water for two or three days when crossing the Desert, during which time they will only receive a small measure of corn or a few dates. On the coast, they are driven hard a long day, sweating, and

But the defeat of the Emperor's eldest son, Sidi Mahomed, at the Battle of Isly, who commanded upwards of forty thousand of these cavaliers, has thrown a shade over the ancient celebrity of this Moorish corps, and these proud horsemen have since become discouraged. On covered with foam, their sides bleeding from the huge sharp-edged stirrups. Without the slightest covering, they are left out the whole night, and their only evening meal is a little chopped barley-straw.

Our European horses would perish under such circumstances, and the French have lost the greater part of the horses they imported from France for the cavalry. But this hard fare keeps down the fiery spirit of these stallion barbs, otherwise they would be unmanageable. When turned out to grass, they soon become wild. Crossing a field one day, mounted, I was set upon by a troop of these wild, grazing horses, and was instantly knocked to the ground, where I lay stunned. A cavalry officer, who was riding with me, had only just time to escape, and saved himself by dismounting, and letting his horse go.

It was some hours before we could rescue the horses of our party from their wild mates, sporting and bounding furiously over the plains. The barb horses being all stallions (for the Moors consider it a crime to geld so noble an animal), the fiercest and most terrific battles ensue on a stud that fatal day, however, none of the black bodyguard of the Emperor was brought into action. These muster some thirty thousand strong. This corps, or the Abeed-Sidi-Bokhari,* are soldiers who possess the most cool and undaunted courage; retreat with them is never thought of. Unlike the Janissaries of old, their sole ambition is to *obey*, and not to *rule* their sovereign. This fidelity to the Shereefs remains unshaken through all the shocks of the empire, and to the person of the Emperor they are completely devoted. In a country like Morocco, of widely distinct races and hostile tribes, all natu-

breaking loose from their pickets. These battles are always between strangers, for the barb is the most affectionate of horses, and if he is known to another, and become his mate, he will, as the Arabs say, " die to be with him."

* These trained bands of negroes call themselves *Abeed-Sidi-Bokhari*, from the patron saint whom they adopted on settling in Morocco, the celebrated Sidi-Bokhari, commentator on the Koran, and a native of Bokhara, as his name implies. His commentary is almost as much venerated as the Koran itself.

rally detesting each other, the Emperor finds in them his only safety. I cannot withhold the remark, that this body-guard places before us the character of the negro in a very favourable light. He is at once brave and faithful, the two essential ingredients in the formation and development of heroic natures.

It will, I trust, not be deemed out of place to consider for a moment the warlike propensities and qualities of the negro. Every European who has penetrated Africa, confesses to the bellicose disposition of the negro, having seen him engaged with others in perpetual conflict. The choice and retention of a body-guard of Blacks by the Moorish Emperor, also triumphantly prove the martial nature of the negro race. But the negro has signally displayed the military qualities of coolness and courage in many instances, two or three of which I shall here take the liberty of mentioning, in connexion with the affairs of Algeria.

Mr. Lord relates, on the authority of the

French, that, when the invading army invested Fort de l'Empereur, and had silenced all its guns, the Dey ordered the Turkish General to retreat to the Kasbah, and leave three negroes to blow up the fort. It seemed, therefore, abandoned, but two red flags floated still on its outward line of defence, and a third on the angle towards the city. The French continued all their efforts towards effecting a practicable breach. Three negroes were now seen calmly walking on the ramparts, and from time to time looking over as if examining the progress of the breach. One of them, struck by a cannon-ball, fell; and the others, as if to avenge his death, ran to a cannon, pointed it, and fired three shots. At the third, the gun turned over, and they were unable to replace it. They tried another, and as they were in the act of raising it, a shot swept the legs from under one of them. The remaining negro gazed for a moment on his comrade, drew him a little aside, left him, and once more examined the breach. He then snatched one of the flags, and retired to the interior of the tower. In a few minutes, he re-appeared, took a second flag and descended. The French continued their cannonade, and the breach appeared almost practicable, when suddenly they were astounded by a terrific explosion, which shook the whole ground as with an earthquake. An immense column of smoke, mixed with streaks of flames, burst from the centre of the fortress; masses of solid masonry were hurled into the air to an amazing height, while cannon, stones, timbers, projectiles, and dead bodies were scattered in every direction. What was all this? The negro had done his duty—the fort was blown up!

In a skirmish near Mascara, one of Abd-el-Kader's negro soldiers killed two Frenchmen with his own hand. The Emir, who was an eye-witness of his bravery, rewarded him on the field of battle by presenting him with his own sword and the Cross of the Crescent, the only military order in the service, and which is never awarded except for a very distinguished action. Colonel Scott says the black was presented to him, and seemed as proud of the honour conferred on him as if he had been made a K.G.C.B.

In the strifes and disputes for succession that have characterized the history of the Barbary princes, and reddened their annals with blood, nothing has been more remarkable than the fidelity of the negroes to their respective masters, and the bravery with which they have defended them to the last hour of their reign or existence. When all his partisans have deserted a pretender, when the soldiers of the successful competitor to the throne have been in the act of pouncing upon the fallen or falling prince, a handful of brave followers has rushed to the rescue, and surrounded the person of their beloved leader, pouring out their life-blood in his defence—and these men were negroes! To use a vulgar metaphor, the negro will defend his master with the savage courage and tenacity of a bull-dog. And this is the principal reason which has induced the despotic princes of North Africa to cherish the negroes, of whom they have encouraged a continual supply from the interior.

The history of this Imperial Guard of Negroes is interesting, as showing the inconveniences as well as the advantage of such a corps, for these troops have not been always so well conducted as they are at present. At one time, the Shereefs claimed a species of sovereignty over the city of Timbuctoo and the adjacent countries. In the year 1727, Muley Ismail determined to re-people his wasted districts by a colony of negroes. His secret object was, however, to form a body guard to keep his own people in check, a sort of black Swiss regiment, so alike is the policy of all tyrants. In a few years, these troops exceeded 100,000 men. Finding their numbers so great, and their services so much needed by the Sultan, they became exigeant and rapacious, dictating to their royal master. Muley Abdallah was deposed six times by them. Finding their yoke intolerable, the Sultan decimated them by sending them to fight in the mountains. Others were disbanded for the same reasons by Sidi Mohammed. Still, the effect of this new colonization was beneficially experienced throughout the country. The Moors taking the black women as concubines, a mixed race of industrious people sprang up, and gave an impetus to the empire. It is questionable, however, if North Africa could be colonized by negroes. By mixing with the Caucasian race, this experiment partly succeeded. But in general, North Africa is too bleak and uncongenial for the negroes' nature during winter. The negro race does not increase of itself on this coast. Their present number is kept up by a continual supply of slaves. When this is stopped, coloured people will begin gradually to disappear.

It is unnecessary to tell my readers that the Shereefs are very sensitive on matters of religion;

but an anecdote or two may amuse them. A French writer expatiating in true Gallic style, calls Morocco the "arrière-garde en Afrique of Islamism," and "une de ses armées de réserve." Indeed, the coasts and cities of Morocco are inundated with saints of every description and degree of sanctity. Morocco, in fact, is not only the *classic* land of Marabouts, but their home and haunt, and sphere of agitation. There are ten thousand Abd-el-Kaders and Bou Mazas all disputing authority with the High Priest, who sits on the green throne of the Shereefs. Sometimes they assume the character of demagogues, and inveigh against the rapacity and corruption of the court and government. At others they appear as prophets, prophets of ill, by preaching boldly the Holy war.

The French in Africa now furnish them with an everlasting theme of denunciation. From Morocco they travel eastwards, filling the Sahara and the Atlas with the odours of their holy reputation. So that religious light, like that of civilization, is now moving from the west—eastwards, instead of, as in times past, from the east—eastwards. The Maroquine Mahometans may be cited as a case in point. They find too frequently only the form of religion in the east, as we do in the eastern churches. They are beginning to assault Mecca as we have assaulted Jerusalem.

Now for an anecdote or two illustrative of the high state of orthodoxy professed by the Shereefs. Some time ago, a number of handkerchiefs were brought, or rather smuggled into Mogador, having printed upon them passages from the Koran. One of them got into the hands of the Emperor, who thinking the Christians were ridiculing the Sacred Book, ordered instanter all the cities of the coast to be searched to discover the offender who introduced them. Happily for the merchant he was not found out. His Highness commanded that all the handkerchiefs which were collected should be destroyed. When Mr. Davidson was at Morocco, he prescribed some Seidlitz water for the use of the Sultan, and placed on the sides of two bottles, containing the beverage, Arabic verses from the Koran. The Sultan was exceedingly exasperated at this compliment to his religion, and had it privately intimated to Mr. Davidson not to desecrate the Holy Book in that abominable manner. The latter then very prudently gave up to the minister all the printed verses he had brought with him, which were concealed from public view. But if some of these emperors are so rigid and scrupulous, there are others more liberal and tolerant.

Muley Suleiman was a great admirer of the European character, and was much attached to a Mr. Leyton, an English merchant. This merchant was one day riding out of the city of Mogador, when an old woman rushed at him, seized the bridle of his horse, and demanded alms. The merchant pushed her away with his whip. The ancient dame seeing herself so rudely nonsuited, went off screaming revenge;

and although she had not had a tooth in her head for twenty long years, she noised about town that Mr. Leyton had knocked two of her teeth out, and importuned the Governor to obtain her some pecuniary indemnification.

His Excellency advised Mr. Leyton to comply, and get rid of the annoyance of the old woman. He resolutely refused, and the Governor was obliged to report the case to the Emperor, as the old lady had made so many partisans in Mogador as to threaten a disturbance. His Imperial Highness wrote a letter to the merchant, condescendingly begging him to supply the old woman with "two silver teeth," meaning thereby to give her a trifling present in money. Mr. Leyton, being as obstinate as ever, was ordered to appear before the Emperor at Morocco. Here the resolute merchant declared that he had not knocked the teeth out of the old woman's head, she had had none for years, and he would not be maligned even in so small a matter.

The Emperor was at his wits' end, and endeavoured to smooth down the contumacious Leyton, to save his capital from insurrection; imploring him to comply with the Lex talionis,* and have two of his teeth drawn if he was inflexibly determined not to pay. The poor Emperor was in hourly dread of a revolution about this tooth business, and at the same time he knew the merchant had spoken the truth. Strange to say, Mr. Leyton at last consented to lose his teeth rather than his money. However, on the merchant's return from the capital to Mogador, to his surprise, and no doubt to his satisfaction, he found that two ship-loads of grain had been ordered to be delivered to him by the Emperor, in compensation for the two teeth which he had had punched out to satisfy the exigencies of the Empire.

* The *lex talion* is frequently enforced in North Africa.

CHAPTER V.

Several visits from the Moors; their ideas on soldiers and payment of public functionaries.—Mr. Cohen and his opinion on Maroquine Affairs.—Phlebotomising of Governors, and Ministerial responsibility.—Border Travels of the Shedma and Hhaha tribes.—How the Emperor enriches himself by the quarrels of his subjects.—Message from the Emperor respecting the Anti-Slavery Address.—Difficulties of travelling through or residing in the Interior.—Use of Knives, and Forks, and Chairs are signs of Social Progress.—Account of the periodic visit of the Mogador Merchants to the Emperor in the Southern Capital.

I RECEIVED several visits from the Moors. As a class of men, they are far superior in civility and kindness to the Moorish population of Tangier. So much for the foolish and absurd stories about the place, which tell us that it is the only city of the Empire in which Christians can live with safety and comparative comfort. These tales must have been invented to please the Tangier diplomatists. The contrary is the fact, for, whilst the Moors of Tangier consist of camel drivers and soldiers, there are a good number of very respectable native merchants in Mogador; nevertheless, a large portion of the population is in the pay of government as militia, to keep in check the tribes of the neighbouring provinces; but their pay is very small, and most of them do a little business; many are artizans and common labourers. As a specimen of their ordinary conversation, take the following.

Moors.—" All the people of Morocco are soldiers; what can the foreigner do against them? Morocco is one camp, our Sultan is one, we have one Prophet, and one God."

Traveller.—" In our country we do not care to have so many soldiers. We have fewer than

France, and many other countries; but our soldiers do not work like yours; they are always soldiers, and fight bravely."

Moors.—" We don't understand; how wonderful! the French must conquer you with more soldiers."

Traveller.—" We have more ships, and our principal country is an island; the sea surrounds us, and defends us."

Moors.—" How much pay has the Governor of Gibraltar?"

Traveller.—" About 20,000 dollars per annum."

Moors.—" Too much; why, the Koed of Mogador is obliged, instead of receiving money, to send the Emperor, at a day's notice, 20, or 30,000 dollars! or if he does not pay, he is sent to prison at once; his head is not the value of a slave's."

It appears that the old governor (who is now in Morocco) positively refuses any salary or presents; his Excellency is a man of some small property, and finds this plan answers best. He will not be fattened and bled as the Emperor treats other governors. He politely hinted this to the Emperor when he accepted office; since then, he has resolutely refused all presents from the merchants, so that the Emperor has no excuse whatever for bleeding him under the pretext that he is afflicted with a plethora, from his exactions on the people. The moneys referred to by the Moors are the custom dues, which are collected by a separate department, and transmitted direct to the Emperor.

Whilst residing at Mogador, Mr. Cohen arrived from Morocco, where he had been with the merchants. He is the English Jew who assisted Mr. Davidson in his travels through Morocco. His experience in Maroquine affairs is considerable, and I shall offer his conclusions concerning the present state of the Empire. I prefer, indeed, giving the opinion of various residents or natives of the country to our own. Mr. Cohen's ideas will be found to differ exceedingly from that of the (Imperial) merchants, who, in point of fact, are not free men, and cannot be trustworthy witnesses. As Mr. Elton justly observed, the Europeans are so much involved with the Emperor, that they are almost obliged to consent publicly to the violent death of the unfortunate Jew, Dorman, although he was under the French protection, and likewise a kind of vice-consul.

Mr. Cohen says—" the people of Morocco are tired of their government, tired of being pillaged of their property, tired of the insecurity and uncertainty of their possessions; that is to say, of the few things which still remain in their hands." Mr. Cohen goes so far as to say—that, were a strong European power to be established on the coast, the entire population would flock to its support. He gives the following instance of the style and manner in which the Emperor bleeds the governors of provinces.

A few years ago, a governor of Mogador presented himself to the Sultan of Fez. He was received with all due honours. The governor then begged leave to return to Morocco. He was dismissed with great demonstrations of friendship. He arrived at Morocco, and the governor of that city immediately informed him that he was his prisoner, the Sultan having a claim against him of 40,000 dollars. At length, the poor dupe of royal favour obtained permission to go back to Mogador and to sell all he had, in order to make up the sum of 40,000 dollars.

This is the way in which things are managed there. Of Maroquine policy, Mr. Cohen says, "That when the Sultan finds himself in a scrape, he gives way, though slightly dilatory at first. So long as he sees that he does not commit himself, or is not detected, he does what he likes with his own and other people's likewise, to the fullest extent of his power. But on any mishap befalling him, Muley Abd Errahman, whenever he can, always shifts the responsibility upon his ministers, and if one of them gives his advice, and the course taken therein does not succeed, woe be to the unhappy functionary!"

Some years ago, a number of troops rebelled against the Emperor. At the instance o the prime minister, Ben Dris, they were pardoned; but, instead of receiving gratefully this imperial mercy, the troops broke out afresh in rebellion, which, with great difficulty, was quelled by the Sultan. This, however, being accomplished, he called the prime minister before him, and thus addressed the amazed vizier.

" Now, Sir, receive four hundred bastinadoes for your pains, and pay me 30,000 ducats; you will then take care in future how you give me advice." Nevertheless, Ben Dris still remained vizier, and continued so till his death. Bastinadoing a minister in Morocco is, however, much the same as a forced resignation, or the dismissal of a minister in Europe. Doubtless Ben Dris thought himself surprisingly lucky that the Emperor did not cut off his head.

It was the late Mr. Hay's opinion, that Muley Abd Errahman was a good man, but surrounded with bad advisers. The probability seems rather, that he took all the credit of the good acts of his advisers, and flung on them the odium of all the bad acts committed by himself, as many other despotic sovereigns have often done before him.

With regard to the disaffection of the people, as alleged by Mr. Cohen, its verification is of great importance to us, and our appreciation of it equally so.

We might be counting upon the resistance of the Maroquines against an invasion of the French, and find, to our astonishment, the invaders received as deliverers from the exactions and tyrannies of the Shereefian oppressor. The fact is, Morocco will never be able to resist the progress of nations any more than China, especially since she has got the most restless people in the world for her neighbours. Besides, during the last thirty years, many of the

Maroquines have visited Europe, and their eyes are becoming opened, the film of Moorish fanaticism has fallen off; even on their aggressive neighbours, they see the exercise of a government less rapacious than their own, and more security of life and property. Still, the Emperor will use every means to build up a barrier against innovation.

Just at this time, a *rekos* (courier) arrived from Mr. Willshire (now at Morocco), bringing letters in answer to those which I had addressed to him, touching my visit to the Emperor. He writes that he had "already received orders from His Imperial Majesty respecting the object of my mission," which words give me uneasiness, as they are evidently unfavourable to it, and consequently to my journey to Morocco.

There is a misunderstanding between the provinces of Shedma and Hhaha. These districts adjoin Mogador, the city belonging to Hhaha. Shedma is mostly lowland and plains, and Hhaha highlands and mountains, which form a portion of the south-western Atlas, and strike down into the sea at Santa Cruz. There seems to be no other reason for those frequent obstinate hostilities on both sides, except the nature of the country. It is lamentable to think, because " a narrow frith" divides two people, or because one lives in the mountains and the other in the plains, that therefore they should be enemies for ever! Strange infatuation of poor human nature.

Here the feud legend babbles of revenge, and says that, in the time of Muley Suleiman, one day when the Hhaha people were at prayers at Mogador, during broad day light, the Shedma people came down upon them and slaughtered them, and, whilst in the sacred and inviolable act of devotion, entered the mosques and pillaged their houses. This produced implacable hatred between them, which is likely to survive many generations; but the story was told me by a Hhaha man, and not improbably the people of

Shedma had some plausible reason for making this barbarous attack.

Even before this piece of treachery of one Mussulman towards another at the hour of prayer, the feuds seemed to have existed. It is a remarkable circumstance in the history of Islamism, that many of the most treacherous and sanguinary actions of Mahometans have been committed within the sacred enclosures of the mosques, and at the hour of prayer. One of the caliphs having been assassinated in a mosque, seems to have been the precedent for all the murders of the kind which have followed, and indelibly disgrace the Mussulman annals.

These Hhaha and Shedma people are also borderers, and fight with the accustomed ferocity of border tribes.

Their conflicts are very desultory, being carried on by twos and threes, or sixes and sevens, and with sticks, and stones, and other weapons, if they cannot get knives, or matchlocks. Meanwhile, the Emperor folds his arms, and looks on superbly and serenely. When the two parties are exhausted, or have had enough of it for the present; his Imperial Highness then interferes, and punishes both by fine. Indeed, it pays him better to pursue this course; for, instead of spending money in the suppression of factious insurrections, he gains by mulcting both parties. The Sultan, in fact, not only aggrandizes himself by the quarrels of his own subjects, but he profits by the disputes between the foreign consuls and his governors.

The imbroglio which took place some years since, between the Governor of Mogador and the French Consul, M. Delaporte, is sufficiently characteristic. An Algerine Mussulman, who was of course a French subject, behaved himself very indecent, by setting all the usual rules of Mahometan worship at defiance. This was a great scandal to the Faithful. The Governor of Mogador, in defiance of religion, took upon himself to punish a French Mussulman. The French Consul remonstrated strongly in presence of the Governor, almost insulting him before his people. The Sultan approved the conduct of his governor. The Consul General decided that both parties ought to be removed, and the French Government recalled their vice-consul. The Sultan, promised, but did not dismiss his Governor, or rather the Governor himself would not be dismissed. The French reiterated their complaints, which were supported by a small squadron sent down to Mogador. The Governor was now cashiered, and was besides obliged to pay the Emperor a fine of thirteen thousand dollars, upon the pretext of appeasing the offended Majesty of his royal master. So the Sultan always makes money by the misadventures of his subjects. To indemnify the poor Governor for his fine, he received soon after another appointment.

On his return from Morocco, having waited upon Mr Willshire regarding the presentation of the Petition of the Anti-Slavery Society, the Vice-Consul explained the great difficulty the Emperor had in receiving a petition which called for an organic change in the social condition of the country, and that, indeed, the abolition of slavery was "contrary to his religion." I then represented to Mr. Willshire the propriety at least of waiting for the arrival of the Governor of Mogador from Morocco, in order to have a personal interview with him, to which the Vice-Consul acceded.

The difficulties of travelling through Morocco; and of residing in the inland towns have been already mentioned.

In further proof, Mr. Elton related that, whilst the merchants visited the Emperor in the southern capital, a watch-maker, a European and a Christian, asked permission of the Minister to dwell in the quarter of the Moors, instead of that of the Jews, in which latter the Europeans usually reside.

The Minister replied, "you may live there if you like, but you must have ten soldiers to guard you." Such a reply from the Minister, and whilst the merchants were protected by the presence of the Emperor himself, is all conclusive as to the insecurity attached to Europeans in the interior towns.

Morocco itself is a city of profound gloom, where the Moor indulges to the utmost his taciturn disposition, and melancholy fatalism. It is, therefore, not an enchanting abode for Europeans, who, whilst there waiting on the Emperor, are obliged constantly to ride about to preserve their health, or they would die of the suffocating stench in the Jew's millah, or quarter. But, in taking this equestrian exercise, they are not unfrequently insulted. An ungallant cavalier deliberately stopped Mrs. Elton by riding up against her.

The lady spurred her horse and caught with her feet a portion of his light burnouse, dragging it away. He was only prevented riding after and cutting her down, by one of the Emperor's secretaries, who was passing by at the time.

Mr. Elton had a fine black horse to ride upon. The populace were so savage at seeing an infidel mounted upon so splendid an animal, that they hooted: "Curse you, Infidel! dismount you dog!"

These instances shew the sauciness of the vulgar, and are a fair example of the conduct of the Moors. I am told by Barbary Jews, it would be next to impossible for a Christian to walk without disguise in broad daylight at Fez. Not so much from the hostility of the populace, as from their indecent and vehement curiosity. However, in these cases, I am obliged to give the testimony of others. Mr. Cohen, when travelling through the interior, assumes the character of a quack doctor, the best passport in all these countries. Practising as he goes, he manages to get enough to bear his charges on the way.

Oliver Goldsmith piped, but in Morocco the traveller and stranger physics his way. To Europeans, Mr. Cohen gives this advice— "Never to stay more than one night at any place." "Mr. Davidson," he says, "stopped so long at Wadnoun, that all the Desert, as far as Timbuctoo, heard of his projects and travels, and were determined to waylay and plunder him."

But, on the contrary, with respect to my own experience in the Desert, the people appeared equally hostile or offended at my taking them by surprise. Desert travelling after all is mostly an affair of luck. Six travellers might be sent to Timbuctoo and three return, and three be murdered, and yet the three who were murdered might have been as prudent and as skilful as the three who were successful. The Maroquine Government often shew a perfect Chinese jealousy of Europeans travelling in the interior. When Doctor Willshire, brother of the Consul, returned from Morocco, the Government gave orders that "he should be taken directly to Mogador, and not be allowed to turn to the right hand or to the left, to collect old stones or herbs." This lynx-eyed government imagined they saw in Doctor Willshire's botanical and mineralogical rambles, a design of spying out the powers and resources of the country.

The consentaneous progress of Morocco in the universal movement of the age, is argued by the merchants from an increased use of chairs, and knives and forks. Some years ago, scarcely a knife and fork, or a chair was to be found in this part of Morocco. Now, almost every house in the Jewish quarter has them. The Jew of Barbary can use them with less scruple than the orthodox Tory Moor, who sets his face like flint against all changes, because his European brethren adopt them. Many innovations of this domestic sort are introduced from Europe into North Africa through the instrumentality of native Jews. Tea has become an article of universal consumption. It is, indeed, the wine of the Maroquine Mussulmen.* Even in re-

* Maroquine Moors drench you with tea! they guzzle sweet tea all day long, as the Affghans gulp down their tea, with butter in it, from morning to night.

mote provinces, amongst Bebers and Bedouins, the most miserable looking and living of people the finest green tea is to be found.

You enter a miserable looking hut, when you are amazed by the hostess unlocking an old box, and taking out a choice tea service, cups, saucers, tea-pot, and tea-tray, often of white china with gilt edges. These, after use, are always kept locked up, as objects of most precious value. The sugar is put in the tea-pot, and the Moors and Jews usually drink their tea so sweet that it may be called syrup. But if any lady tries the plan of melting the sugar while the tea is brewing in the tea-pot, she will find the tea so prepared has acquired a different, and not disagreeable flavour.

Morocco has its fashions and manias as well as Europe. House building is now the rage. They say it is not so easy for the Sultan to fleece the people of their property when it consists of houses. Almost every distinguished Moor in the interior has built, or is building himself a spacious house. This mania is happily a useful one, and must advance the comfort and sanitary improvement of the people. It is as good as a Health of Towns Bill for them.

The merchants having all returned from Morocco, I shall give some account of their visit to the Emperor. The ancient rule of imperial residence was, that the Sultan should sojourn six months in Fez, and six months in Morocco, the former the northern, and the latter the southern capital. This is not adhered to strictly, the Emperor taking up his abode at one capital or the other, and sometimes at Micknos, according to his caprice. He never fails, however, to visit Morocco once a year, on account of its neighbourhood to Mogador, his much loved, and beautiful commercial city. The Emperor himself, before his accession to the throne, was the administrator of the customhouse of this city, where he has acquired his commercial tastes and habits of business, which he has cultivated from the very commencement of his reign. When the Emperor resides in the South, he receives visits from the merchants of Mogador. These visits are imperative on the merchants, if they are his imperial debtors, or even if they wish to maintain a friendly feeling with his government. Upon an average, the visits or deputations of merchants, take place every three or four years; more frequently they cannot well be, because they cost the merchants immense sums in presents, each often giving to the value of three or four thousand dollars. In return, they receive additional and prolonged credits.

The number of Imperial merchants is about twenty, three of whom are Englishmen, Messrs. Willshire, Elton, and Robertson. Most of the rest are Barbary Jews.*

There is a Belgian merchant who did not go

* Native Jews manage most of the business of the interior, and farm the greater part of the monopolies. But the Emperor must have some European merchants connected with these Jews to maintain the commercial relations of his country with Europe. The Jewish High Priest of Mogador is a

with these. This gentleman, owing nothing to the Emperor, preferred to pay duty on shipping his merchandize, on which by payment of ready money, he gets 25 per cent discount. This plan, however, does not enable him to compete with the Imperial merchants, whose duties accumulate till they are years and years in arrear. And when these arrears have gone on increasing till there is no chance of payment, the Emperor, in order to keep up his firms of enslaved merchants, will rather remit half or more of the debt, in consideration of a handsome present, than encourage merchants to make ready money payments. The largest debt owing by a single firm, is that of a native Jew, viz., 250,000 dollars. The amount of the debt of the united Mogador merchants is more than one million and a half of dollars The usual course of the merchants is to pay the debt off by monthly instalments.

merchant, it being considered no interference with his sacred functions.

As an instance of the Emperor's straining a point to keep solvent one of his mercantile firms, on the occasion of the visit of the merchants to Morocco, his Imperial Highness lent the house of Hasan Joseph (Jews) 10,000 dollars in hard cash, which, to my knowledge, were paid to them out of the coffers of the Mogador custom-house. This was certainly an instance of magnanimous generosity on the part of Muley Abd Errahman. But the Emperor's genius is mercantile, and he is determined to support his Imperial traders; and his conduct, after all, is only the calculation of a miser.

It must be mentioned, however, to the honour of Mr. Elton, that on the bombardment of Mogador, he and his lady were allowed to leave at once, having paid up all their government debt. Indeed, the governor of that place, was always accustomed to say to the collector of the returns of the monthly payment of instalments: "Now, go first to Mrs. Elton; she will be sure to have the money ready for you. And we must have money to-day from some of the merchants." On another occasion, his Excellency called the lady of Mr. Elton, "the best man amongst the merchants." Mrs. Elton, being a vivacious, energetic lady, was often called "the woman of the Christians."

The following are the stations at which the merchants stop from Mogador to Morocco, to visit the Emperor.

1st. Emperor's Gardens; five hours from Mogador, where are some fine fig trees, and a spring.

2nd. Aïn Omas.

3rd. Seeshouar.

4th. Wad Enfes.

The country, for the first two days, is beautifully rural, scattered over with noble Argan forests, on the third and fourth days, the journey is through plains and an open country. On the second day, after leaving Mogador, you obtain a distinct view of the great Atlas range at the back of Morocco; on the fifth, as you approach the capital, the country is overspread with wild date-palms, palmettos, or dwarf palms. The view of

"Towering Atlas that supports the sky,"

now stands forth, vaster and more magnificent as you approach the capital, and is the only feature of surpassing interest on the journey; but it suffices to absorb all the attention of the traveller. As he gazes on the giant mountain, which seems to support with its huge rocky arms the frame-work of the skies, its head covered with everlasting snow, he forgets the fatigue of his painful route under an African sun; and, lost in pious musings, adores the Omnipotent being who laid the foundation of this solid buttress.

Half way is called "the Neck of the Camel," where there is a well in the midst of a scene extremely desert and dreary. Here all the donkeys of the party of merchants died from want of water. The water of this well is not permitted to be drunk by animals, in obedience to the solemn Testament of the Saint who dug it. The poor horses and mules were tied close up to the well, looking wistfully at the water when drawn for the biped animals, and snuffing the scent; but they were not allowed to taste a drop. Two horses broke loose and fought, their combat being aggravated by thirst, "See!" cried the Moors to the merchants, "the Saint is angry with you for having wished to give his water to horses."

Our merchants, however, in defiance of the Saint (this invisible enemy of the lower creation) and of his supporters, got a supply of water, which during the night, and *en marche* the next day, they distributed to their steeds. The accommodation on the way, and at the capital is very bad, even the waiting-room near the palace, appropriated to the Christians, is but an old dilapidated shed, with one of its sides knocked out, or never filled in. "Everything," say our merchants, " is going to rack and ruin in the capital. The Emperor will not even repair his palaces, or the jealousies in which he keeps his women; money is his only pursuit and his God."

Their residence in the capital was very disagreeable, all being cooped up in the Jews' quarter, and obliged to subsist on victuals cooked by these people, which made certain of them unwell, for some of the Barbary Jew's food is very indigestible.

The presentation of the merchants to the Emperor was conducted as follows: At nine in the morning, they were admitted into a garden in presence of about two thousand imperial guards, all drawn up in file, looking extremely fierce. Passing these bearded warriors, they were conducted into a large square lined with buildings, where, after waiting about five minutes, the gate of the palace was suddenly thrown open, and the Emperor rode out superbly mounted on a white horse, followed on foot by a group of courtiers. His Imperial Highness was attended by the Governor of Mogador, who walked by his side.

The first persons presented to the Shereefian lord were the officials of Mogador, who were introduced by the Governor of that city; afterwards came some Moorish grandees; then the Christians were presented, and finally the Jewish merchants. The latter were introduced by the Governor of Mogador, the Jews taking off their shoes as they passed before the Emperor. One passed at a time, with his *cadeau* behind him, carried by an attendant Jew. As the merchants moved on, his Imperial Highness asked their names, and condescended to thank each of them separately for his offering.

The merchants carried in their hand, an invoice of their respective presents, and gave it to the Governor, for the articles on their delivery are not exposed before the eyes of the Sultan. To open the budget would be a breach of good breeding, and would shock the Imperial modesty.

Fifteen merchants were introduced, and the ceremony of presentation lasted about twenty minutes; this being concluded, the merchants were permitted to perambulate the gardens of the Emperor, and to pluck a little fruit. They were afterwards delayed a fortnight, waiting to present a *cadeau* to the Emperor's eldest son. Such are the details of this journey, which I got from the merchants themselves. Mr. Willshire, being a consul and great customer of his Imperial Highness, also received a gift of a horse in exchange. The united value of the presents to the Emperor, on this occasion, was fifty thousand dollars, which amply indemnifies him for his money-lending, and the credit that he gives. They consisted principally of articles of European manufactures. His Imperial Highness afterwards sells them to his subjects on his own account. Of course, amongst this mass of presents, there are many nice things such as tea, sugar, spices, essences &c., for his personal comfort and luxury, as well as for his harem, besides articles of dress and ornament.

It will not be out of place here, to give a brief account of the commerce of Morocco. In doing so, we must take into consideration the prodigious quantity of imports and exports, of which there are no statistics in the Imperial custom-houses, and no consular returns. Let us estimate the population of Morocco at its general compensation of eight millions, and suppose that each spends a dollar per annum in the purchase of European manufactures. This will raise the value of imports at once to eight millions of dollars per annum. It is notorious that the contraband trade of Tangier, and Tetuan, and the northern coast generally doubles or trebles the commerce that passes through the custom-house; but the legal trade is not well ascertained.

Mr. Hay once sent, I believe, to the Agent

of Mogador, a list of questions to be answered by the consular department. The gentleman, who was an unsalaried vice-consul, appalled at the number of interrogatories, immediately replied, "That he had his own business to attend to; he could not sit down to compose consular returns, which would require weeks of labour; and if it were considered part of his duties to answer such questions, he begged to resign at once his vice-consulship."

As to the Barbary Jews, who have charge of some of the vice-consulates, they are necessarily incapacitated, by reason of their want of education, for such an employment. It is, therefore, hopeless to attempt to give any accurate account of the commerce of Morocco, I can only annex a few details of those things of which we are actually cognizant.

Whatever may be said of the indolent habits of the Moors, they were once, and still are, a commercial people. Spain, the neighbour of Morocco, still feels the loss of the Moors. They were the really industrious classes settled in Spain. The merchants, the artists, the operatives, and agriculturists unfortunately have left behind them few inheriting their habits of perseverance. Little, indeed, can be expected in Spain, where the maxim is adopted, that "nobility may lie dormant in a servant, but becomes extinct in a merchant." Spain lost upwards of three millions of intelligent and industrious Moors, a shock she will never recover.

The bombardment of a commercial city of this country would not do the injury which is commonly imagined. The ports are numerous though not very good. A single house or shed on the beach of Mogador, or Tangier, is a sufficient custom-house for the Moors. There are no great deposits of goods on the coast, for as soon as the camels bring their loads of exports, these are shipped, and the camels immediately return to the interior, laden with imported goods or manufactures.

Mogador is the great commercial depôt of the Atlantic coast, and therefore "the beautiful Ishweira, the beloved town," of Muley Abd Errahman. Its trade is principally, however, with the south, the provinces of Sous and Wadnoun, and the Western Sahara. Mogador is also the bonâ-fide port of the southern capital of Morocco. Two-thirds of the commerce of Mogador is carried on with England, the rest is divided among the other nations of Europe; but of this third, I should think France has one half. The port of Mogador has usually some half-a-dozen vessels lying in it, but from twenty to thirty have been seen there. They are usually sixty days discharging and taking in cargo. Each vessel pays forty dollars port-dues, which must press very heavily upon small vessels, but it is seldom that a vessel of less than one hundred tons is seen at Mogador. The grand staple exports are only two, gum and almonds; upon the sale of these, the commercial activity of this city entirely depends. English vessels come directly from London, the French from Marseilles; but so badly is this commerce managed that, at the present time, Morocco produce is higher in Mogador than it is in London or Marseilles; for instance, Morocco almonds are cheaper in London than Mogador.

Mazagan, and some few other ports, export produce direct to Europe, but Tangier is the next commercial port of the empire. There is an important trade in manufactures and provisions carried on between Tangier and Gibraltar. The Fez merchants have resident agents in Gibraltar. Curious stories are told of Maroquine adventurers leaving Tangier and Fez as camel-drivers and town-porters, and then assuming the character and style of merchants in Gibraltar, throwing over their shoulders a splendid woollen burnouse, and folding round their heads a thoroughly orthodox turban in large swelling folds of milk-white purity.

In this way, they will walk through the stores of Gibraltar, and obtain thousands of dollars' worth of credit. The merchant-emperor found it necessary to put a stop to this, and promulgated a decree to the effect, that " he would not, for the future, be responsible for the debts of any of his subjects contracted out of his dominions."

This was aimed at these trading adventurers, and the decree was transmitted to the British Consul, who had it published in the Gibraltar Gazette while I was staying in that city. Up to this time, the Emperor, singularly enough, had made himself responsible for all the debts of his subjects trading with Gibraltar.

The trade in provisions at Tangier is most active, bullocks, sheep, butcher's meat, fowls, eggs, game and pigeons, grain and flour, &c., are daily shipped from Tangier to Gibraltar. The garrison and population of Gibraltar draw more than two-thirds of their provisions from this and other northern parts of Morocco.

This government speculates in and carries on commerce; and, like most African and Asiatic governments, has had its established monopolies from time immemorial, of some of which it disposes, whilst it reserves others for itself, as those of tobacco, sulphur, and cochineal. All the high functionaries engage in commerce, and this occupation of trade and barter is considered the most honourable in the empire, sanctioned as it is by the Emperor himself, who may be considered as the chief of merchants. The monopolies are sold by public auction at so much per annum. On its own monopolies, government, as a rule, exacts a profit of cent per cent.

The following is a list of the monopolies which the Emperor sells, either to his own employers or to native and foreign merchants.

1. Leeches.—This is one of the most recently established monopolies, dating only about twenty years back. The trade in leeches was set on foot by Mr. Frenerry; it brought, at first, but a few dollars per annum, and now the monopoly is sold for 50,000. Leeches are principally

found in the lakes of the north-west districts, called the Gharb.

2. Wax.—This monopoly is confined almost exclusively to the markets of Tangier and El-Araish. It sold, while I was in the country, for three thousand dollars.

3. Bark.—This is a monopoly of the north, principally of the mountainous region of Rif. It is farmed for about sixteen thousand dollars.

4. The coining of copper money.—The right of coining money in the name of the Emperor, is sold for ten thousand dollars to each principal city. It is a dangerous privilege to be exercised; for, should the alloy be not of a quality which pleases the Emperor, or the particular governor of the city, the unfortunate coiner is forthwith degraded, and his property confiscated. Indeed, the coiner sometimes pays for his negligence, or dishonesty, with his head.

5. Millet, and other small seeds.—This mono-

poly at Tangier is sold for five hundred dollars. The price varies in other places according to circumstances.

6. Cattle.—The cattle exported from Tetuan, Tangier, and El-Araish, for the victualling of Gibraltar, is likewise a monopoly; it amounted during my stay to 7,500 dollars. In consequence of an alleged treaty, but which does not exist on paper, the Emperor of Morocco has bound himself to supply our garrison of Gibraltar with 2,000 head of cattle per annum, 1,500 of which must be shipped from Tangier, the rest from other parts of the Gharb, or north-west. British contractors pay five dollars per head export duty, the ordinary tax is ten. It is estimated, however, that some three or four thousand head of cattle are annually exported from Morocco for our garrison. The Gibraltar Commissariat contractors complain, and with reason, that the Maroquine monopolist supplies the British Government with "the very worst cattle of all Western Barbary."

These monopolies do not interfere with the custom-house, which levies its duties irrespectively of them. Leeches pay an export duty of 2*s.* 9*d.* the thousand; wax pays an *ad valorem* duty of fifty per cent; bark pays a very small duty, and millet scarcely a penny per quintal.

Independently of these monopolies, there are exports of merchandise of a special character, and requiring a special permission from the Sultan, such as grains and beasts of burden; and, if we may be permitted, bipeds, or Jews and Jewesses.

His Imperial Highness has absolute need of Jews to carry on the commerce of the country. No male adult Jew, or child, can leave the ports of Morocco, without paying four dollars customs duty. A Jewess must pay a hundred dollars. The reason of there being such an excessive export-duty on women is to keep them in the country, as a sort of pledge for the return of their husbands, brothers or fathers, in the event of their leaving for commercial or other purposes. Slaves are not exported from Morocco. Besides the payment of special impost on exportation, wool pays a duty of three dollars per quintal, and two pounds of powder when dirty, and double when washed. A bullock pays export duty ten dollars, and a sheep one. Sheep-skins eight dollars the hundred, bullock-skins three dollars per quintal, and goat-skins the same. Of grain, wheat pays an export duty of three-fourths of a dollar per fanega, or about a quintal. Barley is not exported, there being scarcely enough for home consumption.

Horses are exported in small numbers, by special permission from the Emperor. A few years since when Spain threatened the frontier of Portugal, the English Goverment found it necessary to come to the aid of the latter country, and Mr. Frenerry was commissioned by our Government to purchase of the Emperor five hundred horses for Portugal.

His Imperial Highness called together his governors of cities, and shieks of provinces, and after a long debate, it was unanimously decided that so large a number of horses could not be sold to the Christians without danger to the empire, whilst also, the transaction would be contrary to the principles of Islamism.

Should an individual wish to export a single horse, he would have to pay sixty dollars, a duty which entirely amounts to a prohibition, many of the boasted beasts not being worth twenty dollars. A mule pays forty, and an ass five dollars. Mules are much dearer in Morocco and in other parts of Barbary than horses. Camels are rarely exported, and have no fixed import.

The Queen of Spain, some time ago, solicited the Sultan for four camels, and his Imperial Highness had the gallantry to grant the export free of duty.

There are several exports which are not monopolies. These are principally from the south. The following are some of them.

Ostrich feathers.—These are of three qualities; the first of which pays three dollars per pound, the second quality one and a half dollars, and the third, three-quarters of a dollar. Many feather merchants are now in Mogador visiting at the feasts of the Jews, who reside in Sous and Wadnoun, and have communications with all the districts of the Sahara.

Elephants' teeth.—Ivory pays an export duty of ten per cent. During late years, both ivory and ostrich feathers have lost much of their value as articles of commerce.

Gums.—Gum-arabic pays two dollars per quintal export duty, and gum sudanic an *ad valorem* duty of ten per cent. But now-a-days only the very best gum will sell in English markets; the inferior qualities, as of all other Barbary produce, are shipped to Marseilles. One looks with extreme interest at the beautiful pellucid drops of Sudanic gum, knowing that the Arabs bring some of it from the neighbourhood of Timbuctoo.

Almonds.—Both the sweet and the bitter, in

the shell, or the oil of almonds, pay three dollars per quintal. Ship-loads at once are exported from Mogador direct for Soudan.

Red woollen sashes are exported at five dollars per dozen. The Spaniards take a great quantity. Tanned skins, especially the red, or Morocco, are exported at ten per cent, *ad valorem*. Slippers pay a dollar the hundred. The haik or barracan is exported in great numbers to the Levant by the pilgrims. The vessels, also, that carry pilgrims from Morocco, return laden with these and other native manufactures. Barbary dried peas are exported principally to Spain, paying a dollar the quintal. Fez flour pays one dollar and a half per fanega; dates pay five dollars the quintal; fowls and eggs, the former two dollars per dozen, the latter two dollars per thousand; oranges and lemons pay a dollar the thousand.

Gold is brought from Soudan over the Desert, and is sometimes exported. I have no account of it, and never heard it mentioned in Morocco as an article of any importance.

Olive-oil is exported from the north, but not in great quantities. The amount exported in a recent year was about the value of £6,000 sterling. The olive is not so much cultivated in Morocco as in Tunis and Tripoli.

Besides the articles above mentioned, antimony, euphorbium, horns, hemp, linseed, rice, maize, and dra, orchella weed, orris-root, pomegranate peel, sarsaparilla, snuff, sponges, walnuts, garbanyos, gasoul, and mineral soap, gingelane, and commin seeds, &c., are exported in various quantities.*

It was reported in the mercantile circles, that representations would be made to the Emperor to place the trade of the country upon a regular, and more stable footing. All nations, indeed, would benefit by a change which could not but be for the better. But I question whether his Imperial Highness will give up his old and

* See Appendix at end of Vol. II.

darling system of being the sovereign-merchant of the Empire. It is not the interest of Great Britain to annoy him, for we have always to look at Gibraltar. But it would be desirable if Christian merchants could be found to undertake the duty, to have all the vice-consuls of the coast Christians, in preference to Jews. By having Jewish consuls, we place ourselves in a false position with the Emperor, who is obliged to submit to the prejudices of his people against Hebrews. British merchants ought to be allowed to visit their own vessels whilst in port, to superintend, or what not, the stowing or landing of their goods, as they are entitled to do by treaty.

Spanish dollars are the chief currency in Morocco; but there are also doubloons and smaller gold coins. This currency, the merchants manage very badly. A doubloon loses sixteen pence, or four Maroquine ounces in exchange at Mogador, whilst at the capital of Morocco, three days' journey from this, it passes for the same value it bears in Spain and Gibraltar.

As to the revenues of the Government of Morocco, our means of information are still more uncertain and conjectural, than those we possess regarding commerce. A French writer asserts, that the tithes upon land assigned by the Koran and the capitation tax on the Jews, produce from twenty to thirty million francs (or say about one million pounds sterling) per annum. This, perhaps, is too large a sum.

About a century ago, the revenues of Moocco were estimated at only £200,000 sterling per annum. But if Muley Abd Errahman has fifty millions of dollars, or ten millions sterling in the vaults of Mequinez, he may be considered as the richest monarch in Africa, nay in all Europe. It is positively stated that Muley Ismail left this amount, or one hundred millions of ducats in the imperial treasury, which Sidi Mahommed reduced to two millions. It may have been the great object of the life of the present Sultan to restore this enormous hoard. No country is rich or safe without a vast capital in hand as a reserve for times of trouble, war, or famine. But it is not necessary that such reserve should be in the hands of a government.

This, a Maroquine prince cannot comprehend, and he decides as to the riches and poverty of his country by the amount he possesses in his royal vaults.

In treating of trade, and comparing its exports with the peculiar products and manufactures of the cities and towns, hereafter to be enumerated, we may approximate to an idea of the resources of the Maroquine Empire, but everything is more or less deteriorated in this naturally rich country.

Cattle and sheep, grain and fruits, are of inferior quality, owing to the want of proper culture. No spontaneous growth is equal to culture, for such is the ordinance of Divine Prodence. Half of this country is desert. The iron hand of despotic government presses heavily upon all industry. If we add to this defective state of culture, the miserably moral condition of the people, we have the unpleasant picture of an inferiorly civilized race of mankind scattered over a badly cultivated region. Not all the magnificence of the glorious Atlas can reconcile such a prospect to the imagination. But, unhappily, Morocco does not constitute a very striking exception to the progress of civilization along the shores and in the isles of the Mediterranean. Many countries in Southern Europe are in a state little superior, and the Moorish civilization is almost on a par with that of the Grecian, Sicilian, or Maltese, and quite equal to Turkish advancement in the arts and sciences of the nineteenth century. The only real advantage of the Turks over the Moors consists in the improvements the former have made in the organization of the army. Whoever travels through Morocco, and will but open his eyes to survey its rich valleys and fertile plains, will be impressed with the conviction that this country, cultivated by an industrious population, and fostered by a paternal government, is capable of producing all the agricultural wealth of the north and the south of Europe, as well as the Tropics, and of maintaining its inhabitants in happiness and plenty.

CHAPTER VI.

Influence of French Consuls.—Arrival of the Governor of Mogador from the Capital; he brings an order to imprison the late Governor; his character, and mode of administering affairs.—Statue of a Negress at the bottom of a well.—Spanish Renegades.—Various Wedding Festivals of Jews.—Frequent Fêtes and Feastings amongst the Jewish population of Morocco.—Scripture Illustration, "Behold the Bridegroom cometh!"—Jewish Renegades.—How far women have souls.—Infrequency of Suicides.

NOTWITHSTANDING the sarcasm of a French journalist that the French and other Europeans consuls are "consuls des jusifs, et pour la protection des jusifs," the French consuls both here and at Tangier, have real power and influence with the Government.

The Governor of Mogador, Sidi Haj El-Arby,

arrived from Morocco. His Excellency feared an attack from the Shedma and the Hhaha people, and was obliged to have a strong escort. Not long ago, the Sultan himself had a narrow escape from falling into the hands of a band of insurgents; their object was to make their lord-paramount a prisoner, and extort concessions as the price of his liberty. This will help us to form an opinion of the want of sympathy between potentate and subjects in Morocco.

His Excellency brought an order from the Imperial despot to imprison the late governor, if the balance of 6,000 dollars was not instantly forthcoming, he having only paid nine out of the 15,000 demanded. The late governor was confined in his house, instead of in the common prison. It was said he was worth 30,000 dollars, but that he was afraid to make too prompt a payment of the demand of the Emperor, lest he should be called upon for more. However, his furniture, horses, and mules were sold in the public streets; a melancholy spectacle was the degradation of a former governor of this city."*

* Muley Abd Errahman is averse to treating his governors with extreme rigour. Mr. Hay gives an appalling account of private individuals arrested on suspicion of possessing great wealth—"The most horrible tortures are freely resorted to for forcing confessions of hidden wealth. The victim is put in a slow oven, or kept standing for weeks in a wooden dress; splinters are forced between the flesh and the nail of the fingers; two fierce cats are put alive into his wide trousers, and the breasts of his women are twisted with pincers. Young children have sometimes been squeezed to death under the arms of a powerful man, before the eyes of their parents.

A wealthy merchant at Tangier, whose *auri sacra fames* had led him to resist for a long time the cruel tortures that had been employed against him, yielded at length to the following trial. "He was placed in a corner of the room, wherein a hungry lion was chained in such a manner as to be able to reach him with his claws, unless he held himself in a most unnatural position." This reads very much like a description of the torments of the Inquisition. The Moors may have imported this system of torture from Spain. Similar barbarities were said to have been inflicted by King Otho on prisoners in Greece, even on British Ionian subjects! I recollect particularly the sewing up of fierce cats in the

The Moors look upon these things as matters of course, or with indifference, quietly ejaculating, "It is destiny! who can resist?" but the Moor, nevertheless, can clearly discern that wealth is a crime in the eyes of their sovereign. I am not surprised at the present governor absolutely rejecting all presents, and making the people call him by the *soubriquet* of "the Governor of *no* presents,"

A short time after his appointment, a merchant having left his Excellency a present during his absence from home, was immediately summoned before him, when the following dialogue ensued:—

His Excellency.—"Sir, how dare you leave a present at my house?"

The Merchant.—"Other governors before your Excellency have received presents."

His Excellency.—"I am a governor of *no*

petticoats of women. My experience in Morocco does not permit me to authenticate Mr. Hay's horrible picture.

presents! How much do you owe the Sultan, my master?"

The Merchant.—" I—I—I—don't know," (hesitating and trembling)

His Excellency.—" Very well, when you owe the Sultan nothing, bring me a present, and take this away, and make known to everybody, that Haj El-Arby receives *no* presents."

The fact is, the Governor knows what he is about. Were his Excellency to receive 16,000 dollars per annum as presents from the merchants of Mogador, the Sultan would demand of him 15,999; besides, there is not a merchant who makes a present that does not demand its value, a *quid pro quo* in the remission of custom-duties. Sidi-El-Arby is also a thorough diplomatist, so far as report goes; he promises anybody anything; he keeps all on the tiptoe of most blessed expectation, and so makes friends of everybody. " To his friend, Cohen," he says, " I'll take you back to my country with me, and make you rich; we are of the same country."

To Phillips, " You shall have a ship of your own soon." To the merchants, " The Sultan shall lend you money whenever you want it." To the Moors in general," You shall have your taxes reduced." In this way, his Excellency promises and flatters all, but takes very good care to compromise himself with none.

The frequented as well as the unfrequented spots are centres of superstition. In the Sahara, by a lonely well, in the midst of boundless sterility, where the curse on earth seems to have burnt blackest, a camel passes every night groaning piteously, and wandering about in search of its murdered master, so the tale was told me. Now, about two day's journey from Mogador, there is also a well, containing within its dank and dark hollow a perpetual apparition. At its bottom is seen the motionless statue of a negress, with a variety of wearing materials placed beside her, all made of fine burnished gold, and so bright, that the dreary cavern of the deep well is illuminated. Whoever presumes to look down the well at her, and covets her shining property, is instantaneously seized with thirst and fever; and, if he does not expire at once, he never recovers from the fatal effects of his combined curiosity and avarice. People draw water daily from this well, but no one dare look down it.

Truth may be in this well! since there is a sad want of it on this, as on other parts of the world.

I was introduced to a Spanish renegade, a great many make their escape from the presidios of the North. On getting away from these convict establishments, they adopt the Mahometan religion, are pretty well received by the Maroquines, and generally pass the rest of their days tranquilly among the Moors. I imagine the better sort of them remain Christians at heart, notwithstanding their public assumption of Islamism. This renegade was a stonemason, whom I found at work, and he was not at all distinguishable by strangers from the

Moors, being dressed precisely in the same fashion. I had some conversation with him, which was characteristic of conceit, feeling and honour.

Traveller—" How long have you escaped ?"

Renegade.—" More than twenty years."

Traveller.—" Do you like this country and the Moors ?"

Renegade.—Better is Marruécos than Spain."

Traveller.—" Shall you ever attempt to return to Spain ?"

Renegnde.—" Why ? here I have all I want. Besides, they would stretch my neck for sending a fellow out of the world without his previously having had an interview with his confessor."

Traveller. — " Are you not conscience-stricken ? having committed such a crime, how can you mention it ?"

Renegade.—" Pooh, conscience ! pooh, corazor !"

Many of those wretched men have indeed

lost their corazor, or it is seared with a red-hot iron.

Some hundreds of these Spanish convicts are scattered over the country, but they soon lose their nationality. It is probable that, from some knowledge of them, the Emperor presumed lately to call the Spaniards "the vilest of nations," and yet at various times, the Maroquines have shown great sympathy for the Spaniards. Some of these renegades were found at the Battle of Isly in charge of field-pieces, where, according to the French reports, they displayed great devotion to the cause of the Emperor.

When the governors of the convict settlements find too many on his hands, or the prisons too full, they let a number of their best conducted escape to the interior. The presence of those cut-throats in Morocco may have something to do with such broils as the following, of which I was a witness. Two fellows quarrelled violently, and were on the point of sticking one another with their knives, when up stepped a third party and cried out, "What! do you intend to act like Christians and kill one another?" At the talismanic word of Eusara ("Christians, or Nazareens,") they instantly desisted and became friends. The term "Christian or Nazareen," is one of the most oppobrious names with which the people of Mogador can abuse one another.

The weddings and attendant feasts of the Jews are the more remarkable, when we consider the circumstance of the social state of this oppressed race in Morocco, their precarious condition, and the numberless insults and oppressions inflicted on them by both the government and the people; I was present at several of these weddings, and shall give the readers a glimpse of them. I had read and heard a great deal about the persecution of the Jews in Morocco, and was, therefore, not a little surprised to meet with these continual feasts and festivals among a people so much talked about as victims of Mussulman oppression.

I find two sentences in my notes containing the pith of the whole. "The Jews continued their feasts; about a third of their time is spent in feasting." Again—"Amidst all their degradation, the Jew we saw to-day recreating themselves to the utmost extent of thier capacities of enjoyment." It appears that during the time I was at Mogador there was an unusual number of weddings, and then followed the feast of the Passover. I think, whilst I was at Tangier, weddings or celebration of weddings were going on every night. It may be safely asserted, that no people in Barbary enjoy themselves more than the Jews, or more pamper and gratify their appetites. What with weddings, feasts, and obligatory festivals, their existence is one round of eating and drinking. These feasts, besides, do not take place in a corner, nor are they barricaded from public, or envious, or inquisitorial view, but are open to all, being attended by Christians, Moors and Arabs.

These wedding-feasts are substantial things.

Here is the entry in my journal of an account of them: "A bullock was killed at the house of the bridegroom, tea and cakes and spirits were freely, nay universally distributed there. The company afterwards went off with the bridegroom to the house of the bride, where another distribution of the same kind took place, whilst half of the bullock was brought for the bride's friends. Here the bridegroom, in true oriental style, mounted upon a couch of damask and gold. The bride, laden with bridal ornaments of gold and jewels, and covered with a gauze veil, was led out by the women and placed by his side. She was then left alone to sit in state as queen of the feast, whilst the company regaled themselves with every imaginable luxury of eating and drinking. Her future husband now produced, as a present for his bride, a splendid pair of jewelled ear-rings, which were held up amidst the screaming approbation of the guests. The Jewesses present, were weighed down under the dead weight of a profusion of jewels and gold, tiaras of pearls, necklaces of coral and gems, armlets, wristlets and legets of silver gold and jet, with gold and silver braided gowns, skirts and petticoats.

This fiesta was kept up for seven days. Astonished at the profusion of jewels worn by the various guests, I received a solution by a question I asked, touching this mavellous circumstance. The greater part of the jewels, worn on these occasions, are borrowed from friends and neighbours; they must belong to some of the Jewish families, and their quantity shews the great wealth possessed by the Jews living under this despotic government,

I assisted at the celebration of the nuptials of a portion of the family of the feather merchants, a rich and powerful firm established in the south for the purchase of ostrich-feathers.

This was a wedding of great *éclat*; all the native Jewish aristocracy of Mogador being invited to it. The festivities, beginning at noon, I first entered the apartment where the bride was sitting in state. She was elevated on a radiant throne of gold and crimson cushions amidst a group of women, her hired flatterers, who kept singing and bawling out her praises. " As beautiful as the moon is Rachel !" said one. " Fairer than the jessamine !" exclaimed another. " Sweeter than honey in the honey-comb !" ejaculated a third. Her eyes were shut, it being deemed immodest to look on the company, and the features of her face motionless as death, which made her look like a painted corpse.

To describe the dresses of the bride would be tedious, as she was carried away every hour and redressed, going through and exhibiting to public view, with the greatest patience, the whole of her bridal wardrobe. Her face was artistically painted; cheeks vermillion; lips browned, with an odoriferous composition; eye-lashes blackened with antimony; and on the forehead and tips of the chin little blue stars. The palms of the hands and nails were stained with henna, or brown-red, and her feet were naked, with the toe-nails and soles henna-stained. She was very young, perhaps not more than thirteen, and hugely corpulent, having been fed on paste and oil these last six months for the occasion. The bridegroom, on the contrary, was a man of three times her age, tall, lank and bony, very thin, and of sinister aspect. The woman was a little lump of fat and flesh, apparently without intelligence, whilst the man was a Barbary type of Dickens' Fagan.

The ladies had now arranged themselves in tiers, one above the other, and most gorgeous was the sight. Most of them wore tiaras, all flaming with gems and jewels. They were literally covered from head to foot with gold and precious stones. As each lady has but ten fingers, it was necessary to tie some scores of rings on their hair. The beauty of the female form, in these women, was quite destroyed by this excessive quantity of jewellery. These jewels were chiefly pearls, brilliants, rubies and emeralds.

They are amassed and descend as heir-looms in families, from mother to daughter. Some of the jewels being very ancient, they constitute the riches of many families. In reverses of fortune, they are pledged, or turned into money to relieve immediate necessity. The upper tiers of ladies were the youngest, and least adorned, and consequently the prettiest. The ancient dowagers sat below as so many queens enthroned, challenging scrutiny and admiration. They were mostly of enormous corpulency, spreading out their naked feet and trousered legs of an enormous expanse.

Several dowagers seemed scarcely to be able to breathe from heat, and the plethora of their own well-fed and pampered flesh. We had now music, and several attempts were made to get up the indecent Moorish dance, which, however, was forbidden as too vulgar for such fashionable Jews, and honoured by the presence of Europeans. Not much pleased with this spectacle, I looked out of the window into the patio, or court-yard, where I saw a couple of butchers' boys slaughtering a bullock for the evening carousal. A number of boys were dipping their hands in the blood, and making with it the representation of an outspread hand on the doors, posts and walls, for the purpose of keeping off " the evil eye," (*el ojo maligno,*) and so ensuring good luck to the new married couple.

I then mounted the house-top to see a game played by the young men. Here, on the flat roof, was assembled a court, with a sultan sitting in the midst. Various prisoners were tried and condemned. Two or three of the greatest culprits were then secured and dragged down to the ladies, the officers of justice informing them that, if no one stepped forward to rescue them, it was the sultan's orders that they should be imprisoned. Several young Jewesses now clamourously demanded their release. It is understood that these compassionate maidens who, on such occasions, step forward to the rescue, and take one of the young men by the hand, are willing to accept of the same when it may hereafter be offered to them in marriage, so the contagion of wedding-feasts spreads, and one marriage makes many.

I now proceed to the supper-table of the men, where the party ate and drank to gluttonous satiety. Several rabbis were hired to chant, over the supper-table, prayers composed of portions of Scripture, and legends of the Talmud.

The dinning noise of bad music, and horrible screaming, called singing, with the surfeit of the feast, laid me up for two days afterwards. The men supped by themselves, and the women of course were also apart.

My host, anxious that I should see all, insisted upon my going to have a peep at the ladies whilst they were supping. Unlike us men, who sat up round a table, because there were several Europeans among us, the women lay sprawling and rolling on carpets and couches.

In their own allotted apartments, these

gorgeous daughters of Israel looked still more huge and enormous, feasting almost to repletion, like so many princesses of the royal orgies of Belshazzar. But this was a native wedding, and, of course, when we consider the education of these Barbary women, we must expect, when they have drink like the men, white spirits for protracted hours until midnight, the proprieties of society are easily dispensed with. Happily the class of women, who so kept up the feast, were all said to be married, the maidens having gone home with the bride.

Very different, indeed, was another distinguished wedding at which I had the honour of assisting, and which all the European consuls and their families attended, with the *élite* of the society of Mogador; this was the marriage of M. Bittern, of Gibraltar, with Miss Amram Melek. The bridegroom was the Portuguese Consul, the bride, the daughter of the greatest Jewish merchant of the south, and consequently the Emperor's greatest and most honoured debtor. The celebration of this wedding lasted fourteen days.

On the grand day, a ball and supper were given. All the Moors of the town came to see the Christians and their ladies dance. Our musician, or fiddler, kept away from some petty pique, and we were accordingly reduced to the hard necessity of making use of a drum and whistling, both to keep up our spirits and serve up the quadrilles. We had, however, some good singing to make up for the disappointment. His Excellency the Governor intended to have honoured us with his presence, but he gave way to the remonstrance of an inflexible marabout, who declared it a deadly sin to attend the marriages of Jews and Christians.

The marriage guests were of three or four several sets and sorts. There was the European coterie, the choicest and most select, graced by the presence of the bride; then the native aristocrats, and here were the gorgeous sultanas and Fezan spouses; then the lesser stars, and the still more diminished.

Finally, the " blind, the lame, and the halt," surrounded the doors of the house in which the marriage-feast was held, receiving a portion of the good things of this life. The whole number of guests was not more than two hundred. Plenty of European Jewesses shone as bewitching stars at this wedding; but all *param* to us poor Christians. Indeed, there is as little as no love-making, and match-making amongst the isolated Nazarenes; for, out of a population of some fifty European families, there are only two marriageable Christian ladies.

The bride is frequently fetched by the bridegroom at midnight, when there is a cry made, " behold, the bridegroom cometh; go ye forth to meet him!" (Matt xxv—6). This ancient custom prevails most among the Moors. Once, whilst at Nabal, in Tunis, I was roused from my sleep at the dead of the night by wild cries, and the discharging of fire-arms, attended with a blaze of torches. The bridegroom was conveyhis bride to his home. A crowd of the friends of the newly-married couple, followed the camel which carried the precious burden; all were admitted to the feast in the court-yard, and the doors were shut for the night.

At the wedding of the lower classes of the Jews, after dancing and music, there is always a collection made for the bride, or the musicians. On these occasions, the master of the ceremonies calls out the names of the donors as they contribute to the support of the festivities. I was somewhat taken by surprise to hear my name called out, Bashador Inglez (English ambassador) when I attended one of the weddings. But the fellow, making the announcement, attracted my attention more than his flattering compliment. He was dressed in Moorish costume with an immense white turban folded round his head .I could not conceive the reason of a Moor taking such interest in feasts of the Jews.

The secret soon transpired. He was a renegade, who had apostatized for the sake of marrying a pretty girl. His heart is always with his brethren, and the authorities good-naturedly allow him to be master of the ceremonies at these and other feasts, to preserve order, or rather to prevent the Jews from being insulted by the Mahometans.

There are always a few Jewish renegades in large Moorish towns, just enough, I imagine, to convince the Mahometans of the superiority of their religion to that of other nations; for whilst they obtain converts from both Jews and Christians, and make proselytes of scores of Blacks, they never hear of apostates from Islamism. The manner, however, in which these renegades abandon their religion, is no very evident proof of the divine authority of the Prophet of Mecca. Here is an instance.

A boy of this town ran away from his father, and prostrated himself before the Governor, imploring him to make him a Mussulman.

The Governor, actuated by the most rational and proper feeling, remarked to the boy, "You are a child, you have not arrived at years of discretion, you have not intellect enough to make a choice between two religions." The boy was kept confined one night, then beaten, and sent home in the morning.

Another case happened like this when the boy was admitted within the pale of Islamism. Jewish boys will often cry out when their fathers are correcting them, "I will turn Mussulman!" A respectable Jew, who related this to me, observed, "were I to hear any of my sons cry out in this manner, I would immediately give them a dose of poison, and finish them; I could not bear to see my children formed into Mussulman devils."

It really seems the vulgar opinion among the Jews and Moors of this place, that females have no souls. I asked many women themselves about the matter; they replied, "We don't care, if we have no souls." A Rabbi observed, "It women bear children, make good wives, and live virtuously and chastely, they will go to heaven and enjoy an immortal existence; if not, after death, they will suffer annihilation."

This appears to be the opinion of all the well-educated. But a Jewish lady who heard my conversation with the Rabbi, retorted with spirit: " Whether I bear children or not, if my husband, or any man has a soul, I have one likewise, for are not all men born of us women?"

All, however, are well satisfied with this life, whatever may happen in the next; male and female Jews and Mussulmen hold on their mutual career with the greatest tenacity. I made inquiries about suicides, and was told there were never any persons so foolish as to kill themselves.

"We leave it to the Emperor to take away a man's life, if such be the will of God!" and yet the Moors are habitually a grave, dreamy and melancholy people. No doubt the light, buoyant atmosphere keeps them from falling into such a state of mental prostration as to induce suicide.

I now found that many people looked upon me, in the language of the Jewish renegade, as an ambassador, and some went so far as to say, " I can make war with the Emperor if I like ;" others persisted in saying " I am going in search of the murdered Davidson." A man took the liberty of telling Mr. Elton. " A very mysterious Christian has arrived from the Sultan of the English. The Governor hearing that he had ordered a pair of Moorish shoes, sent word to the shoemaker to be as long about them as possible. This Nazarene is going to disguise himself as one of us, in order to spy out our country."

The Moors are certainly a timid and suspicious race. They feel their weakness, and they are frightened of any Christian who does not come to their country on commercial pursuits, as a sportsman, or in some directly intelligible character.

CHAPTER VII.

Interview with the Governor of Mogador, on the Address of the Anti-Slavery Society.—Day and night side of the Mission Adventure.—Phillips' application to be allowed to stand with his "shoes on" before the Shereefian presence.—Case of the French Israelite, Darmon, who was killed by the Government.—Order of the Government against Europeans smoking in the streets.—Character of Haj Mousa, Governor of Mazagran.—Talmudical of a Sousee Jew.—False weights amongst the Mogador Merchants.—Rumours of war from the North, and levy of troops.—Bragadocio of the Governor.—Mr. Authoris's opinion on the state of the Country.—Moorish opinions on English Abolition.—European Slavery in Southern Morocco.—Spanish Captives and the London Ironmongers Company.—Sentiments of Barbary Jews on Slavery.

I HAD an interview by special appointment

with His Excellency the Governor of Mogador regarding the address to be presented to the Shereefian population from the Anti-Slavery Society. I may at once premise that from what I heard of Mr. Hay's diplomatic powers and influence with the Sultan, as well as the peculiar situation in which Mr. Willshire was placed, encumbered with great liabilities to his Highness' custom-house, I already abandoned all hopes of success, and even thought myself fortunate in being able to obtain an interview with the Governor of this commercial city. To have expected anything more, would have been extremely unreasonable on my part, under such circumstances.

It will be as well if I give the address in this place.*

* "To his Imperial Majesty the Emperor of Morocco, Sidi Muley Abd Errahman.

"May it please your Majesty,

"A Society in England, having for its object the Abolition of Slavery and the Slave Trade throughout the world, and denominated the British and Foreign Anti-Slavery Society,

Friday was appointed, being a quiet day, and the Mussulman Sabbath, when His Excellency had little business on hand. The Moors usually being informed of the pacific intentions and friendly disposition of your Majesty towards our Sovereign Queen and Government, and being informed likewise, that your Majesty, in diplomatic relations with other Foreign Princes and States, has universally manifested the greatest desire to preserve peace amongst nations, and, of necessary consequence, the happiness of the human race, are encouraged to approach your Majesty, and to plead on behalf of a numerous and important class of your subjects, the negro and other black slaves.

"These are a people always faithful to their friends and protectors (a most conspicuous and immediate proof of which is seen in your Majesty's Imperial Guard, formed principally of this class of your faithful subjects,) and exhibiting under suffering and oppression the greatest patience and fortitude, yet, during the long course of bygone centuries, they have been subjected to horrid cruelties and barbarities, in order to pander to the vices and to satiate the avarice of their oppressors.

"Now we, the Society in England aforesaid, address your Majesty for the succour and protection of this cruelly oppressed portion of the human race, and in order that you may be graciously pleased to remove the chain of bondage from off these unfortunate victims of the violence and cupidity of devote the morning of their sabbath to prayer, and afternoon to business and amusement. Our wicked men, who, in defiance of all justice and mercy, claim them as their property, and buy and sell them as cattle.

"We further entreat that your Majesty would be graciously pleased to place the slaves in your Imperial dominions upon a footing of equality with the rest of your faithful subjects, and to make them free men, having the rightful possession of their own persons, and being at liberty to travel whithersoever they will.

"For your Majesty rightly understands and knows as well as we do, that God the Almighty Maker of us and you, has made all men equal, and has not permitted man to have property in his fellow man, which reduces them to the level of brutes; therefore, to make slaves of our fellows, our brothers and sisters, is to sin against the will and mind of God, and to provoke his wrath and indignation against us, and against our children after us.

"Consequently, we, the Society in England, aforesaid, in common with some of your own Mussulman sovereigns and people, hold Slavery, and the Slave Trade in extreme abhorrence, because it kills and destroys our brothers whom we ought to love and cherish, because it makes them like brutes, whom we ought to esteem as reasonable beings, because it hardens our own hearts and makes us cruel towards our fellows, whom we ought to treat with kindness and compassion, and because it deforms God's creatures, party consisted of myself, Mr. Willshire, the

in whom we ought to revere his spiritual likeness, man being made after the likeness of God, in possessing a spiritual reasoning soul; these evils, however, are the direct and inevitable consequences of the accursed Slave Trade, and for such reasons we, the people of England in general, abhor it, and seek, in every legitimate and righteous way, to persuade men of every nation in the world to abandon this inhuman and wicked traffic.

"Finally, we implore your Majesty to be pleased to follow out that great act of confidence which you have exercised towards the negro race, in appointing them the life-guards of your Imperial person, by graciously liberating them from the cruel yoke of slavery. From our hearts we believe that your Majesty will find such a spontaneous act of compassion towards the desolate African Slaves to be the wisest worldly policy, and most agreeable to the will of the Eternal Creator of us all. Your loyal subjects will love the goodness of your heart the more, and serve you the better, while all Africa, of which the immense dominions of your Majesty form so large a part, will catch new life and vigour, under the blessing of the Almighty, and grow happy and prosperous in the ages to come.

"Signed and sealed on behalf of the Society in England for abolishing Slavery and the Slave Trade throughout the world.

"(Signed)   THOMAS CLARKSON. (L.S.)"

British Vice-Consul, and Mr. Cohen as interpreter.

About four o'clock P.M. we found the Governor quite alone, telling his rosary of jet beads, squatting on his hams upon the floor of a little dirty shop, not more than eight feet by six in dimensions, with a ceiling of deep hanging cobwebs which had not been brushed away for a century.

A piece of coarse matting was spread over the ground floor, and a sheepskin lay on it for his Excellency to repose upon, but no furniture was to be seen. There was indeed an affectation of nakedness and desolation. Pen and ink were placed by his side, and a number of official papers were strewn about, with some letters bearing the seal of the Emperor. This shop (or reception room) was situate in an immense gloomy square; it was the only one open, and here were the only signs of life.

The Governor had forbidden any of his subjects to be present at the audience, unwilling and afraid lest any should hear a whisper of the question of abolition in the orthodox States of his Imperial Master. Sidi Hay Elarby was an elderly man, with a placid and intelligent countenance. His manners throughout the interview were those of a perfect Moorish gentleman. The Governor could not be distinguished from the people by his dress. He wore a plain white turban, plain burnouse and a pair of common slippers. In such state, we found the the highest functionary of this important city.

His Excellency began by asking me how I was, and welcoming me to his country. I then handed a written speech to the interpreter, who, being a Jew, pulled off his shoes, and crouching down before the Governor, read to him paragraph by paragraph. Each passage was further discussed and replied to by the Governor with energy, nay with vehemence. The interview lasted till dark—nearly two hours.

The following is a copy of the written speech, which was read for the purpose of introducing the Address, and supplying topics of conversation.

"May it please Your Excellency, the mission with which I am charged to this country is to persuade his Imperial Majesty, the Emperor of Morocco, to co-operate in any way which his Imperial Majesty may deem proper, with the people of England for the abolition of slavery. I am sent to the Court of Morocco by a Society of English gentlemen, whose object is to persuade all men, in all parts of the world, to abolish the traffic in human beings, as a traffic contrary to the rights of men and the laws of God.

"In undertaking this mission, these gentlemen applied to the government of our Sovereign Queen to furnish me with letters of recommendation to the British Consuls of this country, the representatives of her Majesty the Queen of England. Copies of these letters are in the possession of Mr. Willshire. Those letters express strong sympathy for the objects of the mission, and require the Consuls to give me their fullest protection; and so far, our gracious Queen, the government, and the English people, are all agreed that it is a good thing to address his Imperial Majesty the Emperor of Morocco, to co-operate with and to assist them in putting down the traffic in slavery in every part of the world.

"If the government of the Queen had thought that they should recommend to your Excellency and your royal master anything contrary to your religion, they could not have given me letters of introduction to their consuls in this country. Rest assured that the English people believe it to be agreeable to the doctrines and precepts of all religions to abolish the traffic in human flesh and blood.

"I pray, therefore, your Excellency to receive the petition, of which I am the bearer, from the Society of English gentlemen. Our Government have already spent three hundred millions of dollars, the money of the people of England, to destroy the traffic in human beings; every day our government continues to spend vast sums, adding to this ernormous amount for the same object of humanity. I am sure that, if your Imperial Master value the friendship of England and the British government, if it be a politic and good thing for Morocco to be allied with the most powerful Christian nation in the world, the most certain way to conciliate and found this alliance on a durable basis, is to co-operate with the people of England for the abolition of the traffic in slaves, and graciously to receive this address from the Society of Abolitionists in London.

"We come not to your Excellency with force of arms—this could not be just; we use only moral persuasion. Our religion disapproves of compulsion in all such affairs. But I can assure your Excellency that the English people will never cease, though all nations be against them, as long as God Almighty holds them up as a people, to endeavour in every possible way, to persuade and convince the world that the traffic in human beings is a great crime."

The Governor replied in these terms:

"Your mission is against our religion, I cannot entertain it or think of it, in any way whatever. If, in other countries, the traffic in slaves is contrary to the religion of those countries, in this it is not; here it is lawful for us to buy and sell slaves. Mahomet, our Prophet, has authorized us to do this; but, at the same time, our slaves must be fed and clothed like ourselves. If you wish a proof of this, you can go and look at my slaves," (pointing to his house). "To be holders of slaves, is a merit with us.

"Your address ought to come directly from your Government, from your Queen to our Sultan. It is not enough that it is recommended by your Government. The European sovereigns are accustomed to act by the advice of their counsellors and ministers; but the Sultan of Morocco always acts without advice or councils.* If the address had come from the Queen, it would have been received, and an answer would have been returned accordingly. Then if your Government had been offended at the answer of my master not agreeing with their opinion, they could have taken their own satisfaction in any way they might have thought proper (or have made war on us).

"The money which you say the people of England have spent for the suppression of the Slave Trade, has been, according to our opinion and religion, misspent, and employed to destroy a system of which we approve, and consider lawful. Still, I hope God will give your country more money to spend, and in abundance.

"The English people and the people of Morocco have been, from time immemorial, great friends, proofs of which I can give you. The guns that we get from other Christian nations, are never

---

* This is not exact. The vizier is often the author of certain lines of policy.

so good as those we get from England. Besides, we always give the English whatever they ask for. When the French were at war with Spain and wished to take Ceutra from her, the English demanded from our Sultan, a small island near Ceutra, to prevent the French from landing and seizing Ceutra. To this request, my Sultan acceded; and to show you that the English are our particular friends, the English gave the island back to us when the war was at an end."

Mr. Willshire now endeavoured to present the Address of the Anti-Slavery Society, praying his Excellency to accept it.

On which, the Governor continued with his usual vivacity, "No; I am sorry I cannot accept it; if I do, the Sultan must also, for now I act as the Sultan. Indeed, I dare not receive the address, nor write to our Lord* about it.

---

* All the Moorish Sultans are spoken of by the people as *Seedna*, "Our Lord," and departed Saints are addressed by the same title.

Nor can I look at it, for in case the Sultan asks me about it, I must swear that I have not touched nor seen the Address. If I look at it, and then say I did not look at it, the Sultan will order my tongue to be cut off from the roof of my mouth.

"And further, O Consul! O Stranger! were our Lord to agree with your Society, and abolish the traffic in slaves throughout his dominions, all the people would rise up against him in revolt, and the Sultan would be the first to have his head cut off.

"Therefore, as a good and wise man, O Stranger—which you must be, or you would not be entrusted with this mission—comply with the orders of the Sultan's message, given to you by me and your Consul.

" Any thing which you want for yourself or your private use, I will give it you, even to the whole of this city of Mogador. But for myself I cannot comply with the prayers of the address, or receive it from your own or the Consul's hands."

The message of the Sultan alluded to, was in substance to give up the attempt of abolishing slavery in Morocco, and not to think of going to the South, but to return at once to England.

The Governor was greatly pleased with the sound of his own voice, and the skill of his argumentations, and has the character of being a loquacious and reasoning diplomatist.

This was the public or day side of the mission; there was also the night side; for where the curiosity of the Moor is excited, it must be gratified, by fair or other means. It was not surprising, therefore, that the wily Shereef should wish to know what this Address of an English Society was, or could be; and if possible to obtain a copy, although for the sake of the people it was found necessary to repudiate alogether its acceptance. Accordingly, the next day, Cohen told me a friend of the Emperor's was anxious to have some conversation with me, and he begged me to take with me the Address.

It was past ten at night, when alone, with my Moorish guide, I found myself treading the long narrow streets of Mogador.

The wind howled and the watch-dogs barked; it was so dark that we could scarcely grope our way, no human being was about; we went up one street and down another, stealing along our way; as if on some house-breaking expedition; and I began to feel suspicious, fearing a trap might be laid for me. Still, I had confidence in the honour of the Moors, I said to my guide.

" When shall we reach your master's?"

Guide.—" God knows; be quiet!"

We continued going through street after street. It was now bitter cold, and a few drops of rain fell from the cutting wing of the north wind.

To my Guide again.

" Where is the house?"

Guide.—" Follow me, don't talk!"

After we had passed other streets, "Is this the street?"

Guide.—" Eskut! (hold your tongue)."

We now entered a low dilapidated gateway, with a broken panelled door, groaning on its hinges.

Again I questioned my guide. "Who lives here?"

Guide.—" Mahboul Ingleez (mad Englishman) hold your tongue! Do you think we Mussulmans will eat you?"

We passed through several court-yards, by the aid of a lantern, which the guide found in a corner, and then entered a corridor. Here he grasped me by the arm, in such wise as made me believe I was about to have my head thrust through a bowstring. I ejaculated; "Allah Akbar! Mercy upon us!" blending Arabic and English in my fright, and struggling, fell with the guide against the door at the end of the passage with a considerable crash. A voice was heard from within. "*Ashbeek* (what's the matter?)" My guide returned, "*Hale* (open)."

A huge negro now laid hold of me, and pulled me up a pair of narrow stairs which led to a species of loft, in a detached portion of the house. The case containing the Address fell out of my hands, and was picked up by the guide. Another apartment within the loft was now opened, shewing, through a dim and indistinct light, a venerable old Moor, sitting in the midst of heaps of papers and books, like a midnight astrologer, or a secret magician. On our entrance, the solitary Moor raised his eyes, quietly, and said faintly, " Where is it?" My guide now rushed in, began talking volubly, and made this harangue, thinking, however, I could not understand him from the rapidity with which he declaimed.

"Sidi," he said, "this Christian is a frightened fool—and a *baheen* (ass)—I had the greatest trouble to get him here—he was frightened out of himself—and now Allah! Allah! I have to take him back again."

I received the compliment in silence, and endeavoured to recover my tranquillity. But I could not help remarking the contrast between my noisy and agitated guide, and the grave manner and immoveable quietness of the recluse. The guide then handed him " the Address," and the Cid opened the box or case with extreme caution, as if it had contained some mysterious spell. The Cid now looked up for a moment at the big negro, who decamped instantly and returned with a teapot and two cups. The two cups were then filled with tea, one of which was presented to me, but I had some hesitation about drinking it. The Cid, looked up at me with a quiet smile, and gently muttered *Eshrub!* (drink,") I drank the tea and then waited anxiously to know what was coming next. The Cid continued to unroll the Address. When this was done, he rolled it up and again unrolled it, and stared at its Roman characters. He eyed the seal and ejaculated, *Haram!*" to himself! alluding, I suppose, to the figure of the slave in chains, it being prohibited to make figures. The Cid now paused a moment, then looked at me again, and finally turning to the Guide said, "*Imshee El-Ghudwah* (go to-morrow, I'll see.)"

The guide now grasped me again by the hand, scarcely allowing me to bow a good night to the Cid, and led me back to my lodgings, where I arrived at midnight. When I awoke in the morning, I really imagined I had been dreaming an ugly dream, until one of the English Jews called, and said he was making a translation of the Address to be dispatched to the Emperor at Morocco, and afterwards he would bring the Address back. The Address was returned to me about a week afterwards, but whether an Arabic translation was ever sent to the Sultan, I know no more than the reader.

Mr. Phillips has applied to the British Vice-consul to know whether, in case of his going up to Morocco to carry a present for the Belgium merchants, here, Phillips, being a Jew, will be obliged to pull off his shoes, which would be depriving him of the rights of British-born subjects, who stand with their shoes on in the Shereefian presence. The Consul says he cannot answer the question, and must send a dispatch to Mr. Hay. Mr. Willshire complimented Phillips: " Ah Phillips, you are always proposing to me some knotty question. You profoundly perplex the mind of Mr. Consul-general Hay.

This leads me to notice the affecting case of the Israelite, Darmon, at one time the French Vice-consul at Mazagran. This young Darmon was fond of Moorish women, and always intriguing with them. Hay Mousa, Governor of Mazagran, reported him to the Emperor, and his Highness sent orders to have him decapitated. It was said afterwards by the Maroquine Government, that " The order was merely to bring him to Morocco, and that, when being conveyed as prisoner, and after attempting to run away, the soldiers of his escort shot him." The Moorish Government also pretend that Darmon attempted first to shoot the guards who shot him, in self-defence.

With regard to his being a French Consul, it is said by the French Government, that he was not their consul at the time, having resigned. It appears besides that members of his family are French, and others Moorish subjects. Indeed, these Mauro-European Jews give great troubles to the consuls; the various persons of a single family being often under the protection of three or four consuls. It will thus be seen how full of difficulties was this Darmon affair, and what a door it opened to tedious Moorish diplomacy. The French Government arranged ultimately with the Sultan a compromise, a sum of money being paid to the murdered man's family, and the Governor of Mazagran was dismissed.

When young Darmon fell into disgrace, his father, one of the Imperial merchants, was at Morocco. The father inquired of the Minister whether the Sultan would receive his present now his son had fallen into disgrace. The cruelly avaricious tyrant deigned to accept it of the father it is said, at the very moment when the order to decapitate his son had been sent to Mazagran. No doubt it was a barbarous action, but the extreme imprudence of the young man provoked the government to extremities. The court was so irritated at the time, that it even issued an order to place all Jews, natives, foreigners, or Europeans upon the same level of exposure to Moorish insult and oppression. Speaking to Mr. Willshire about this order, he smilingly observed: "Say nothing, it will soon be forgotten." The government never intended to carry it out. Years ago, the Emperor gave orders that Jews coming from European countries should be placed on the same footing as native Jews, but the Imperial edicts were unnoticed.

A curious order was given about smoking some time ago in this city. It was represented to the Governor that during Ramadan, Kafer-Nazarenes went about smoking, occasioning the Faithful to sniff up the smoke, and so break the Holy Fast. The Christians were likewise accused of going near the mosques to fill them with filthy smoke.

The Governor, in a circular, begged of the Consuls to prohibit their countrymen, or " subjects," from smoking in the streets. The French Consul considering this a police regulation, summoned together the French subjects, and begged of them to comply with the non-smoking order. Mr. Willshire took no notice of the affair, knowing it would soon pass over.

Mr. Willshire is a veteran in Morocco, and understands the genius of its government. He considers the *laissez faire* system the very best, and this is all very well, provided the Sultan respects the heads of Her Majesty's subjects.

Haj Mousa, Governor of Mazagran, who was mixed up with the Darmon affair, deserves notice from his brutal ferocity towards Europeans. With great difficulty and damage to their lives, Europeans reside in Mazagran, and it is not therefore surprising that the imprudent Darmon fell into the clutches of this provincial tyrant, who probably ensnared him as a prey. Up to the time of this affair, Haj Mousa had been an irremoveable governor. The Sultan himself never attempted to displace him, although he had committed, from time to time, the greatest enormities. Other governors had been bled, fleeced, and impaled over and over again; but the caitiff, Haj, always remained in possession of the fruits of his tyranny.

The reason for this tolerant conduct of the Emperor towards him is, that when Muley Abd Errahman was in difficulties and obliged to fly for his life, in the convulsions previous to his reign, Haj Mousa sent the young prince a mule and thirty ducats; with this, the prince was enabled to escape, and he saved his life to be afterwards proclaimed Meer-el-Moumeneen. On receiving the mule and money, he exclaimed in a transport of gratitude to the Governor of Mazagran, " I will never forget you!" It is unfortunate the good faith of the Emperor's word has been so deplorably abused by this tyrant, for it is considered certain, that though temporarily removed from Mazagran, he will return, or be made governor of another city.

A Sous Jew called upon me one day, who is well acquainted with the Shelouh or, Berber of the South. On asking if he would make a translation of the book of Genesis from Hebrew into Shelouh, he replied :

" No, I cannot. In the first place, the Emperor would cut off my head for doing such a thing; and, again, it would be a sin to convert the Holy Hebrew character into such a language of Infidels."

We continued our discussion on a more practical subject.

Traveller (to the Jew)—" I am told that among you, Jews of Morocco, it is a merit to rob us Christians and the Moors. Your young children are even praised by their mothers if they commit a theft without being found out :* is this right?"

The Jew.—" You are all *Goyeem** (Gentiles), but it is not true that we rob you, Christians. If we rob Mussulmen, it's because they rob us first."

The case really is, the Jews are literally being robbed every day by the Moors one way or the other, and, if the people do not rob them, the constituted authorities continue to make exactions under every pretence. I am inclined, nevertheless, to think, without prejudice, that

---

* It is curious to see the Spartan principle of theft developing itself under such different circumstances.

it is a received maxim with *all native* Barbary Jews, "to rob unbelievers, Moors and Christians, when you can do so *safely*." This was the opinion which a very respectable European Jew, resident in Tunis, entertained of his brethren. At the same time, there are numerous exceptions.

Many of the lower classes of Moors likewise, think there is little or no harm in robbing Jews and Blacks, that is, all who are Infidels and Christians.

I may mention, in connection with the above, the system of False-Weights, which is an enormous scandal to this great commercial city. It appears that almost every tradesman, and every imperial merchant have two sets of weights, one to buy and another to sell with. A merchant once had the impudence to cry out to his clerk when weighing, "Oh, you are wrong, these are my *selling* weights; bring me my *buying* weights. Am I not buying?"

A Jew, once purchasing oil from a poor Arab,

carried his villainy so far as actually to make his tare and tret weigh more than the skin-bag when full of oil, and coolly told the amazed Arab he had no money to give him for the value received. "Give me back my oil!" cried the Arab. At this the audacious Jew retorted, "There is none!" A European merchant interfered, and saved the Jew from the bastinado he so richly deserved. A Kady hearing of these abominations, took upon himself to begin a reform, and went about examining weights. For his honest pains, and, in the midst of his work of reform, the officious functionary received an order from the Sultan, enjoining him to cease his interference, and condemning him, as a punishment for his over-righteousness, *to teach twelve little boys to read every day, and not to sit at his own door for the space of one year.*" So unthankful, so odious is the task of reforming in Morocco and many other countries.

This account of the abominable system of two

kinds of weights, I derived from most unquestionable authority, otherwise I could not have given credit to the statement.

There were incessant rumours of war from the North. The Emperor had got himself into difficulties with Spain and France. Orders had been sent down to reinforce this garrison and that of Aghadir. The day before, the Governor, calling his troops before him, did not shew his usual good sense and prudence. He thus harangued them :—" Now, let those who want new arms come and take them, and bring back the old ones. Let all have courage, and fear not the Christians; fear not, women and children!" The movement of troops was part of a general measure, extending to all the coasts, and was, in fact, a review *en masse* of the disposable forces throughout the empire. Eighty thousand men were expected in this city or the suburbs. The Sultan was reported to be on the march towards the North with an army of 200,000 men.

The Sultan did not expect to make use of his new levies, but the policy of the thing was good. His Highness is evidently a pacific ruler, he has but few regular troops, and he pays them badly. His predecessor had a large army and paid them well.

Great discontent prevailed among the soldiers, and the Emperor never feels himself secure on his throne.

This apparent crusade against the Infidels has no doubt tended to make him popular, and to consolidate his power. True, it excited the tribes of the interior against the Christians, but it was better to inflame them against the Christians than to lose his own throne.

The French Consul waited upon the Governor for explanations about the movements of the troops. His Excellency observed, "I am ordered by my Sultan to defend this city against all assailants, and I shall do so till I am buried beneath its ruins. Though all the coast-cities were captured, Mogador should never be surrendered."

Some of the credulous Moors said, " The Shereefs will come from Tafilet, led on by our Lord Mahomet, and destroy all the cursed Nazarenes. The Sheerefs will fire against the French leaden balls, and silver balls. " Another observed to me, " If a fleet should come here, it will be immediately sunk, because our Sultan has ordered every ball to hit, and none to miss."

This is not unlike what a Turk of Tripoli once said to me about the Grand Signor and his late reforms. " The Turks will soon be civilized, because the Sultan has given an order for all the Turks to be civilized." The large guns of the forts were practised, and the guns of the grand battery loaded. The infantry continued to practise on the beach of the port : their manœuvres were very uncouth and disorderly, they merely moved backwards and forwards in lines of two deep. The French Consul, Monsieur Jorelle, discontinued his usual promenade, to prevent his being insulted, and so to avoid the the painful necessity of demanding satisfaction.

Mr. Willshire, being well known to the Mogador population, had not so much to fear. Here is the advantage of a long residence in a country. The French Government lose by the frequent changing of their consuls. Still, M. Jorelle was right in not exposing himself to the mob, or the wild levies who had come from their mountains. The fault of the Governor was, in exciting the warlike fanaticism of the tribes of the interior against the Christians, which he ought to have known the city authorities might have extreme difficulty in keeping within bounds. No European could pass the gates of the city without being spat upon, and cursed by the barbarous Berbers.

I paid a visit to M. Authoris, the Belgium merchant, and the only European trader carrying on business independently of the Emperor. He represented the commerce of the country to be in a most deplorable condition. " There is now nothing to buy or sell on which there is a gain of one per cent. The improvidence of the people is so great that, should one harvest fail, inevitable famine would be the result, there not being a single bushel of grain more in the country than is required for daily consumption. Nor will the people avail themselves of any opportunity of purchasing a thing cheap when it is cheap; they simply provide for their hourly wants. They act in the literal sense of ' Take no thought for the morrow, but let the morrow take care of itself.' As to the Jews, they feast one day and fast the next." With regard to the excitement then existing, M. Authoris observed. " This Government, on hearing rumours of Spanish and French expeditions against the country, must naturally make use of what power it has, the Holy War power, to excite the people in their own defence. The Moors cannot discriminate Gazette intelligence. When a worthless newspaper mentions an expedition being fitted out against Morocco, the Emperor immediately sees a fleet of ships within sight of his ports, and hears the reports of bombarding cannon."  The raw levies of Shedmah and Hhaha continued to enter the town, but only a small number at a time, lest they should alarm the inhabitants. They went about, peeping into houses, and wherever a door was open they would walk in, staring with a wild curiosity.

I had some conversation with my Moorish friends respecting the abolition of slavery. An old doctor observed, "The English are not more humane than other nations, but God has decreed that they should destroy the slave-trade among the Christians. This, however, is no praise to them, for they could not resist acting according to the will and mind of God. As for the Mussulmen, what they do is for the benefit of slaves, especially females, who, one and all, are doomed to death;* but, when purchased by the

* This is the old story of the abettors of the slave-trade in all parts of the world; I very much doubt if there be

slave-dealers, their lives are spared, and they are made True Believers. Still, the Mussulmen would assist the English in destroying the ships which carry slaves;" (as if the Moors had any fleet).

The number of slaves in this city is from eight hundred to one thousand. It is difficult to ascertain any thing like the exact number, the opulent Moors having many negress slaves, with whom they live in a state of concubinage. Young, rich, and fashionable Moors, I was told for the first time in a Mahommedan country, have become disgusted with the old habit of managing and taking a wife early, and adopt the immoral practice of buying female slaves, by which they avoid, as they say, the trouble and expense of marrying females of their own rank in Moorish society. A good Mussulman must however, marry once in his life. Slaves are

any truth in it. None of the slave-dealers of the Desert whom I conversed with, had ever seen or heard of prisoners of war being put to death.

imported *viâ* Wadnoun from Timbuctoo and Soudan, and even from the western coast. Negroes of the Timbuctoo market are more esteemed than those of Guinea, being a stronger and more laborious race. The common price of a slave in Mogador is from 60 to 90 ducats; one day a beautiful African girl, freshly exported from the interior, was sold for 160 ducats, or about £20 sterling. This is considered an extraordinary high price.

Slaves are sold by criers about the streets in Morocco, and most towns, and not in bazaars, as in the East. But the most remarkable feature of slavery in this part of the world, is the Christian or European slavery carried further south, in the regions extending on the line of coast below Wadnoun, and the adjacent Sahara. Something like a regular system of Christian slavery is there going on, whilst its head-quarters are not more than five or six days' journey from this residence of the European Consuls. This white slavery consists in seizing shipwrecked sailors, numbers being fishermen from the Canary Islands. We know little about these poor captives, although we are so near Wadnoun, and are continually trading with Sous and this country. Mr. Davidson casually mentions them in his journal.

It is a settled and religious practice of merchants to keep Europeans ignorant of the south and the Desert; we only hear of these captives now and then, when one escapes, and after being bought and sold by a hundred different masters, is fortunate enough to be redeemed; of his companions in shipwreck, the escaped captive rarely knows anything. They are gone: they are either drowned near the coast, plundered and massacred, or carried far away into the Desert, and perhaps for ever. Formerly vessels navigated through the channel (if it may be so called) of the Canary Islands and the Wadnoun coast, by which they often got on shoal water, and were cast away; in this manner, whites were enslaved. Happily now, masters of vessels have become acquainted with this dangerous coast. They pass to the east of the Canaries, and fewer vessels are shipwrecked hereabouts.

The Spanish fishermen of the Canaries are chiefly now made captives. These poor people are either seized when becalmed near the coast, or captured on being cast on shore by the furious trade-winds, which sweep these desolate shores (often nine months out of twelve) and carry utter destruction with them. The wild and wandering Bedouins in bad weather, with the true storm scent of the wrecker, patiently watch the coasts, pouncing on their prey, with the voracity of the vulture, as it is thrown up from the deep, along the inhospitable shore. Having got the shipwrecked men in their possession, they act with the cunning and avarice of slave-dealers, and are aided by the still craftier Jews, who always render it very difficult for the consular agents to redeem these unhappy captives. For although a Jew, by the Mahometan law, cannot purchase slaves, yet by buying them through Mussulmen, who share in the profits, from the Arabs who first seized the captives, the slaves are frequently kept back months in the Desert, being parted from one another before they can be ransomed.

Sometimes the Arabs alluringly question their captives to see if they understand any mechanical arts, which are greatly esteemed, being very useful in these almost tenantless regions; and should they discover that they do, they carry them away into hopeless captivity, through the wilds of the Desert, refusing to sell them at any price or offer of ransom. But those who cannot, or will not make themselves useful, are generally redeemed by the Mogador Consuls, should they escape being massacred in the quarrels of the Arabs for the booty when they are first captured.

There is, at the present time, a Spanish fisherman near Wadnoun, waiting to be redeemed. The Arab Sheikh who holds him, demands two hundred dollars for his redemption. Mr. Willshire objects to the price, as being too much. Besides this, he is afraid to advance any money for a Spanish captive's release, lest it should never be refunded. The Spanish Government, representing a people so chivalrous in bygone times, and so proud of their ancient exploits over the Moors of this very country, are not now-a-days over zealous in redeeming their countrymen held in bondage by these people. Mr. Willshire ransomed a Spanish boy, and waited several years before he could get this imbecile Government to refund the money. Espartero at last, however, interfered authoritatively for the repayment to our generous consul.

In the present case of the poor fisherman, the captive Spaniard lingers between hope and fear, his only protection being the avarice of his master, who, like all slave-dealers, is willing to take care of him as he takes care of his horse. He is one out of four, the other three having been massacred by the Arabs, or perished on the coast. But, at present, we know nothing certain of this, although but a few days' journey from the scene where the disaster took place—so miserable are our means of information for enabling us to put an end to this system of Christian slavery. Certainly some representations should be made to the Emperor, who pretends to have jurisdiction over Wadnoun, and the adjacent countries, that these captives may be delivered up to the Consuls of Mogador. A fair remuneration might be given to the persons bringing them safely to this town.

I am told, the Ironmongers' Company of London have at their disposal funds for the liberation of such British captives as are enslaved in Southern Morocco. This money was left by a merchant who himself was made a slave there; and since that time, owing to the few British captives redeemed, it has increased to an enormous amount. Not knowing what to do with the money, the Company, it is said, are about to petition Parliament to build a school with a portion; but I should suggest that it would be more in accordance with the original object, and declared intention of the benevolent donor, were this large surplus fund devoted to the redemption of all other Christian captives, of whatever nation or country. Because two hundred dollars are not forthcoming which could easily be supplied from the Ironmongers' Company's funds, a poor Spaniard is condemned to a cruel and hopeless slavery, wandering in the wilds of the great African wilderness. It is impossible to tell the number of Christian slaves who perish in the South of Morocco. Many of the Consular agents of this city are as ignorant of the country as persons residing in London. This subject absolutely demands the attention of the governments of Europe. Our humanity and civilization are in question.

The opinions of the Jews here, are the same as those of American slave-holders, with this slight difference, that they consider it right to make slaves of white men and Europeans, as well as of black men, negroes, and Africans, in which idea they are more consistent than their Yankee men-selling brethren.

As there are many Barbary Jews at Mogador, more or less under British protection, I took the liberty of reminding them of their liabilities as British subjects, by circulating among them copies of Lord Brougham's Act.

I had some conversation with Rabbi-El Melek and other Jews about the question of abolition,

Traveller.—"What is the opinion of the Jews of this country on the matter of slavery?"

Rabbi-El-Melek.—"I will show you," (taking the Hebrew Bible he read) "'Cursed be Canaan; a servant of servants shall he be unto his brethren.'"

Traveller.—Admitting the curse pronounced here was right, that Ham and Canaan were the progenitors of the African negroes, and that the curse was to be extended to all generations of Africa—are these reasons why the all-Merciful Deity will hold man guiltless who enslaves and maltreats poor Africans? Now, the Jews have been dispersed all over the world, and maltreated, if not enslaved, by both Christians and Mahometans (as now) according to prophecy, but will God hold us guiltless for persecuting or maltreating you, Jews?"

The Rabbi.—" But we are the slaves of God, not of you Christians, and besides, we are commanded to treat well our slaves in the Scriptures." Here he quoted many passages from the Pentateuch.

Then followed a desultory conversation, some asserting "that inasmuch as the slavery of the whites was permitted by God, how much more right had they to enslave blacks who were the servants of servants!" Others even added, "If we were Sovereigns of Morocco, we should make slaves of both Mahometans and Christians." This indeed is the genuine feeling of Barbary Jews; oppression begets oppression, and wrong begets revenge. Another observed, " If you ask me what I think as a British subject, and not as a Jew, I will give you my opinion against slavery."

Such distinctions in morals are not easily admissable, but the Jews there are acute enough to make them, and are as good Jesuits as those of Rome. Some cited the cavtivity of Josephus, as a reason for carrying on the slave-trade.

On another occasion, I had a conversation with Hassan Yousef, the High Priest, or Archbishop, as Captain Phillips calls him. The Chief Priest acknowledged that he who stole a man, whether white or black, was condemned to death, according to the fair interpretation of the Mosaic law. He and all Jews were much astonished at the tenor of Lord Brougham's Act, and got not a little frightened; for all the merchants of Mogador, Christians and Jews, more or less aid and abet the slave-trade, all having connections with slave-dealers. At length, our Jewish Archbishop opined. " Well,

well, it is better now, since the Christians have put down slavery in most of their countries, that we Jews should follow their example."

It would be useful, and might subserve the cause of civilization, were the Jews of Europe to take some means of enlightening their brethren of North Africa on the question of slavery. The Israelites, who have suffered so much from slavery and oppression, after becoming free themselves, should endeavour to emancipate those who are still in the chains of bondage.

The Hhaha levies were about to return to their country; the disposable force of this province is about 70,000. The troops from Shedma were to come in after the departure of those of Hhaha. Government were afraid to bring both together, lest they should fight among themselves. Alluding to the quarrel of their Sultan with the French, these hostile tribes mutter to each other, "We must kill our own French first;" that is to say their own hereditary enemies."

I went out to see the two levies. These tribes had a singularly wild and savage aspect, with only a blanket to cover them, which they wrap round and round their bodies, having neither caps on their heads, nor shoes on their feet. They were greatly excited against the Christians, owing to the foolish conduct of the Moorish authorities. The lawless bands spat at me, and every European passing by them, screaming with threatening gestures, "God curse you! Infidels." These semi-savages, called out for the defence of the Empire, were merely armed with a bad gun or matchlock; some had only knives and clubs. Such levies are certainly more fit to pillage the Emperor's coast-towns than to defend his territory against the foreign enemy.

These poor tribes bring their own provisions, a little barley meal, and olive or argan-oil, or liquid butter; on this being exhausted, they could stay no longer, for Government supplies them with nothing but bad matchlocks.

They were loud in their complaint on not receiving any nations, and threatened to join the French Nazarenes when they arrived. His Excellency the Governor was very anxious to get rid of them, which was not at all surprising. So avaricious is the Emperor, that when he can, he makes the rich Moors supply arms for their poorer brethren, instead of furnishing them from government depôts. And this he insists upon as a point of religion. The Governor called upon rich Moors to supply the poor with arms.

A friend of mine who understands Shelouh as well as Arabic, overheard a characteristic quarrel between a Shedma man and a Hhaha man. The Shedma people, or inhabitants of the plains, mostly speak Arabic, those of the mountains, Shelouh, which difference of language embitters their quarrels, and alienates them from one another.

Shedma man.—"Dog! you have put your hands of the devil into my bag of barley."

Hhaha man.—Dog and Jew, you lie!"

Shedma man.—"Jew and Frenchman! there's some one now in your wife's tent."

Hhaha man.—" Religion of the Frenchman! your mother has been dishonoured a thousand times."

The maternal honour is the dearest of things amongst these semi-barbarians. At the mention of this libel on his mother, the Shedma fellow rushed at the Hhaha man, seizing him by the throat, and unsheathed a dirk to plunge into his bowels. The scuffle fortunately excited the instant attention of a group of Arabs close by, who, securing both, carried them before the Shiekh; who, without hearing the subject of the quarrel, bastinadoed them both with his own hand. But he was the Hhaha Sheikh, and the Shedma Sheikh complained to the Governor of his man having been bastinadoed by the other

Sheikh. The Governor dismissed them, each threatening the other with due vengeance.

It is time to give some account of Mogador. We sometimes spell the name with an *e*, Mogadore, the inhabitants call their town *Shweerah*. Square,* in allusion to its beauty, for it is the only town constructed altogether on geometrical principles throughout Morocco. Its form, however, is really a triangle. Mogador is a modern city, having been built in the year 1760 of our era, by the Sultan Sidi Mohammed, under the direction of a French engineer of the name of Cornut, who was assisted by Spanish renegades.

The object of Sidi Mahommed was to found a central emporium of the commerce of the Empire, and a port for the southern capital (Morocco). This town belongs to the province of Hhaha, whose Berber tribes are its natural defenders.

* The European name of Mogador, is supposed to be derived from Mugdul, or Modogul, a Moorish Saint.

The site is a sandy beach with a rocky foundation or a base on the sea, forming a peninsula, and is supposed to be the ancient Erythræa. The houses are regularly built, with streets in direct lines, extremely convenient though somewhat narrow. The residences of the consuls and European merchants are elegant and spacious. There is a large market-place, which, on days when the market is not held, furnishes a splendid parade, or " corso" for exercising cavalry.

The city is divided into two parts; one division contains the citadel, the public offices, the residence of the governor, and several houses occupied by European consuls and merchants, which are all the property of the Sultan; and the other is the space occupied by the houses of the Moors and Jews.

The Jews have a quarter or *willah* to themselves, which is locked up during the night, the key being kept by the police. Nevertheless, several Jews, especially Imperial traders, are allowed to occupy houses in the Moorish quarter or citadel portion of Mogador, with the Christian merchants.

Both quarters are surrounded by walls, not very thick or high, but which are a sufficient protection against the depredations of the mountaineers, or Arabs of the plain. The port is formed by a curve in the land and the isle of Mogador, which is about two miles from the mainland.

This isle, on the verge of the ocean, contains some little forts and a mosque, and its marabout shrines sparkle in the sun. It is a place of exile for political offenders. When the French landed, at the bombardment of Mogador, they released fifty or sixty state prisoners, some of whom had been Bashaws, or ministers of this and former reigns. The isle, however, is finely situate off the Atlantic, fanned and swept by healthy gales, and the prisoners suffer only seclusion from the Continent. The exiles never attempt to escape, but quietly submit to their destiny.

In the port, there are only ten or twelve feet of water at ebb tide, so that large vessels cannot enter, but must lie at anchor a mile and a half off the Western battery, which extends along the north-western side of the port. Such vessels do not lie there except in the summer months, and then with extreme caution, being, as they are, right off in the Atlantic, on one of its most dangerous coasts. There are some tolerable batteries, but they cannot long resist a European bombardment, which was demonstrated by the French.

Colonel Keating says, " As far as parapets, ramparts, embrasures, cavaliers, batteries, and casemates constitute a fortress, this town is one; but the walls are flimsy, the cavaliers do not command, the batteries do not flash, and the casemates are not bomb-proof. The embrasures are so close that not one in three upon the ramparts could be worked, if they were mounted, which they are not. All their guns, which have been only twelve months here, are already in very bad order, from exposure to the climate and surf. The casemates are so damp, that their interior is covered constantly with a thick nitrous incrustation." Nevertheless, the Moors have such a superstitious veneration for fortifications built by a parcel of renegades, that they will not permit Christians to walk on these ramparts. But what is most unfortunate for the defence of Mogador, the water could be instantly cut off by destroying its aqueduct.

The population is between thirteen and fifteen thousand souls, including four thousand Jews, and fifty Christians, who carry on an important commerce, principally with London and Marseilles. Excepting Tangier, it is now the only port which carries on uninterrupted commercial relations with Europe.

Mogador is situate in the midst of shifting sand-hills, that separate it from the cultivated parts of the country, which are distant from four to twelve miles. These sands have an extraordinary appearance on returning from the interior; they look like huge pyramidal batteries raised round the suburbs of the city for its defence. The inhabitants are supplied with water by means of an aqueduct, fed by the little river, or rill of Wal Elghored, two miles distant south. The climate hereabouts is extremely salubrious, the rocky sandy site of the city being removed from all marshes or low lands, which produce pestiferous miasma or fever-exhaling vegetation. Rarely does it rain, but the whole tract of the adjoining country, between the Atlas and the sea, is tempered on the one side by the loftiest ranges of that mountain, and on the other, by the north-east trade winds, blowing continually. Mogador is in Lat. 31° 32′ 40″ N., and Long. 9° 35′ 30″ W.

The environs offer nothing but desolate sands, except some gardens for growing a few vegetables, and a sprinkling of flowers, which, by dint of perseverance, have been planted in the sand of the sea-shore. This is a remarkable instance of human culture turning the most hopelessly sterile portions of the world to account. These sands of Mogador are only a portion of a vast and almost interminable link, which girdles the north-western coast of the African continent, and is only broken in upon at short intervals, from Morocco to Senegal, like a shifting, heaving, and ever-varying rampart against the aggressions of the ocean. Both wind and sea have probably equally contributed to the formation of this vast belt of shifting sands.

The distance from Tangier to Mogador, by ordinary courier, is twelve days, but no traveller could be expected to perform the journey in less than twenty days.

Other courier distances are as follows:

Tangier to Rabat	4 days
Rabat to Fez	2 ,,
Fez to Mickas	12 hours
Rabat to Morocco	8 days
Mogador to Morocco	$2\frac{1}{2}$,,

Mogador to Santa Cruz . . 3 days
Mogador to Wadnoun . . 8 „
Santa Cruz to Teradant . . 1½ „

A notice of the interesting, though now abandoned part of Aghadir, may not be out place here. Aghadir, (called also Agheer and by the Portuguese, Santa Cruz) means in Berber "walls." It is the Gurt Luessem of Leo Africanus. The town is small, but strong, and well fortified, and is situate upon the top of a high and abrupt rock, not far from the promontory of Gheer, which is the western termination of the Atlas, and where it dips into or strikes the ocean.

On the south, close by, is the river Sous, and formerly Aghadir was the capital of this province.

Aghadir has a spacious and most secure port, which is the last port southwards on the Atlantic. Indeed, this bay is the finest roadstead in the whole empire. Mr. Jackson says, that during his residence at Aghadir of three years, not a single ship was lost or injured. The principal battery of Aghadir, a place equally strong by nature and art, is half way down the western declivity of the mountain, and was originally intended to protect a fine spring of water close to the sea. This fort also commands the approaches to the town, both from the north and the south, and the shipping in the bay.

Santa Cruz was converted from a fisherman's settlement into a city, and was fortified by the Portuguese in 1503. Muley Hamed el-Hassan besieged it in 1536 with an army of fifty thousand men, and owing to the accident of a powder-magazine blowing up and making a breach, the Sultan forced an entrance, to the astonishment of the Portuguese, who were all slaughtered.

In the reign of Muley Ismail, Santa Cruz was the centre of an extensive commerce carried on between Europe and the remotest regions of

Africa, which obtained for it the name of Bab-el-Soudan, (Gate of Soudan.) The inhabitants became rich and powerful, and, as a consequence which so frequently happens to both the civilized and the barbarian, insolent and rebellious. In 1773, Sidi Mohammed was obliged to march out against the town to crush a rebellion; and this done with great slaughter, he ordered all the European merchants to quit the place and establish themselves at Mogador. The father of this prince had sworn vengeance against the haughty city, but died without accomplishing his sanguinary threats. The son, however, did the work of blood, so faithful to vows of evil and violence is man. Since that period, Aghadir has dwindled down to nothing, six hundred inhabitants, and others say only one hundred and fifty. The greater part of these are Jews, who have the finest women in all the country. Mr. Davidson says the population of Aghadir is forty-seven Mohammedans, and sixty-two Jews. At Fonte, the port, are about two hundred

Moors. Were any European power to conquer Morocco, Aghadir would certainy be re-established as the centre of the commerce in the south. To a maritime nation like England, the repair and re-opening of its fine port would be the first consideration, and doubtless a lucrative and extensive commerce could be established between Aghadir and Timbuctoo. The city is seven leagues south of Cape Gheer, in latitude 30° 35'.

I shall now give some further details illustrative of the state of negro slavery. The Emperor has an entire quarter of the city of Morocco appropriated for his own slaves, the number of whom, in different parts of the empire, amounts to upwards of sixty thousand. This is his, the lion's share. His Imperial Highness, who was accepting presents from various governors, lately received five hundred slaves from the Sheikh of Taradant. The trading Moors, believing me to be sent by the British Government to purchase and liberate all their slaves, have calculated the whole of the slaves in Morocco to be worth *twenty-seven millions of dollars.*

A Moor observed, " I hope to see any calamity befall the country rather than that of the slaves being liberated." He observed: " God shews his approbation of slavery by not permitting slaves to rise against their masters, or the free negroes to invade Morocco, who are infinitely more numerous. The reason why the English abolished slavery is because the Queen of England has a good heart, but Mussulmen treat their slaves well, and do not fear the anger of God." When I mentioned that the Bey of Tunis and the Imaum of Muscat had entered into treaties for the suppression of Slavery, the traders observed, " Amongst the Mohammetans are four sects, but the only orthodox sect is that of Morocco."

There is, however, one class of abolitionists in this country—the women, or Mooresses. The rumour that a Christian had come to purchase all the slaves of Mogador soon penetrated the harems. The wife of one of the most distinguished Moors of Mogador informed a Jewess of her acquaintance, that she was very happy to hear a Christian was come to purchase all her husband's slaves, for she was tired of her life with them. The truth is, respectable Moorish females detest this system of domestic slavery, and wish to see it abolished, notwithstanding that they are bred in it, and are themselves little better than slaves. They see themselves gradually abandoned by the husbands of their youth for the most ignorant and degraded negress slaves, whom their husbands purchase one after another as their caprice or passion excites them, until their houses are filled with these slaves.

The artful negress absorbs all the affection of her master, whilst the legitimate wife is left as a widow, and is obliged to wait upon these pampered slaves, whose insolence knows no bounds. The negress slaves besides, when they bear sons, are treated with great respect; their children are free by the law, and cannot be disposed of, although the Moors do sell them when hard pressed for money. Yet even these negresses are beginning to chatter and clatter about the Anti-Slavery mission, expressing their satisfaction to our Jewish neighbours. A negress slave on hearing that a person had come from England to liberate all the slaves, jumped up and called on God to bless the English nation.

This excitement in the domestic circles of Mogador raises the bile of the slave-dealers. A fellow of this sort beckoned me to come to him as I was passing in the street, and thus began: "Christian, if you dare attempt to go to the south, we shall cut you up into ten thousand little pieces."

Traveller.—"You will not lay a finger upon me, nor throw a handful of sand in my face unless it please God."

Slave-dealer.—(Taken aback at this reply, he

drew in his horns), "Well, how much will you give us apiece for our slaves."

Traveller.—"I shall give you nothing; you have no right to sell a man, a brother, like yourself."

Slave-dealer.—"It's our religion."

Traveller.—"It's not your religion to sell Mussulmen; you sell the children of your own slaves, born in your houses, and who are Mussulmen?" The slave-dealer, puzzled and angry, was silent a few minutes, and then said, "Ah, well, all's right, all's from God."

I received a visit from a Hajee under peculiar circumstances. Passing through Tunis on his return from Mecca last year, his slave, hearing that all the slaves were liberated in the country, ran away. In vain his master attempted to catch him. There were no Christians in the country of the Mecca imposter, who kept *man-hunting hounds*. This is the peculiar glory of Christian lands. Tunis is not so "go a-head" as Yankee freedom-land. The consequence was the pilgrim left without his slave. He then, strange to say, applied to me to procure him back his slave. Thinking this a good opportunity to agitate the authorities here on the question, I recommended him to apply to the Governor, who should write to the Emperor, and also to the Bey of Tunis, and so forth. I had visitors daily who asked me when I should be ready to purchase the slaves and liberate them. Arabs from the remotest districts came to me; and I was told that there is not a town or district of the empire, but has heard of the English going to liberate all the slaves of Morocco.

I have studiously avoided giving details of the cruelties and hard bondage of slavery in and around Morocco. On the contrary, I have stated it to be the opinion of the Europeans and Consuls in Tangier, that slaves are well treated in this country. Such an opinion ought to weigh with all.* At the same time, in self-

* The Governor of Mogador told me to go to look at his

defence, as an abolitionist, and occupied with a mission for the extinction of slavery in this country, I must partly uplift the veil, however disgusting it may be to my readers. A portion of the dark side of the picture must be exhibited. Of the march of slave-caravans over the Sahara, I shall say nothing—that is fully reported in my previous publication. When the slaves arrive in Morocco, they are marched about in different directions of the country for sale. During their passage through a populous district like this, where the females are exposed to the brutal violence of ten thousand casual visitors, or agents of police and government, it is the ordinary and revolting practice to adopt means one cannot describe for the purpose of preserving their honour. Private punishments are frequent; to my certain knowledge, a female slave was tied up by the heels, head downwards,

slaves, and see that they were well fed and well clothed. But every rich man's horses and dogs are well-fed and well-housed.

and, after being cruelly flagellated, was left for dead by her pitiless master. She was at last cut down at the intercession of her mistress whose humanity got the better of her hatred and jealousy. While I was at Mogador, a negress had two of her children torn away from her to be sold at Morocco, to pay the debts of her master, who was a Moor. The chlidren were sons of the man who sold them into bondage! The mother was inconsolable, ran about distracted, and probably will never recover from the blow. These facts are enough, and with any human man they will out-weigh all other instances, however numerous, of alleged good treatment on the part of Moorish slave masters.*

---

* Mr. Davidson did not visit Morocco as an abolitionist. Read what impression this Maroquine slavery made upon his mind. "My heart sickens at the sight of this horrid picture. In another lot of these unfortunate beings were six women, one of whom had given birth to a child on the road, which was thrown into the bargain. There was an old wretch who had come from Saweirah to purchase

I took a ride with Mr. Elton on the sandy beach. There is a fort in ruins, at about half an hour's distance, illustrating most emphati-

female slaves; his examination was carried on in the most disgusting manner, I could not refrain from calling down the curse of Heaven on these inhuman wretches. In many, but little feeling is shewn for the poor blacks; and they seemed to think less of their own fate than I did, who was merely a looker-on. One poor creature, however, who was a finer woman, and less black than the rest, shed tears. I could have given her my dagger to have plunged it in the breast of the villain who was examining her. And yet these people pray four times a day, and think themselves superior to all God's creatures! More than ever do I wish to get away from this den of hell-hounds. Each of the grown persons was in the prime of life, and had once a home, and was more to be pitied than the children, who had never known the liberty of thought and act. To each of the ten slaves was given a lunch of bread; while both the inhuman buyers and sellers, after chuckling over their bargains, went to offer up their prayers to Heaven, before they took their daily meal. Can such unhallowed doings be permitted to endure longer! Oh, Spirit of Civilization, hither turn your eyes, and punish the purchasers who ought to know better, for thus only will the sale be stopped."

cally the parable of the man who built his house upon the sands.

This fort, which was to command the southern entrance of the harbour, is supposed to be of Spanish construction, and built about the same time as the city.

It was once of considerable size and height, but is now a fallen and ruined mass, its foundations "upon the sands" having given way. Storms along this shore are often terribly destructive, we passed a portion of the hulk of a vessel completely buried in the sand.*

Notwithstanding the sober and taciturn cha-

---

* I asked a Moor, "Who built this castle on the sands?" He replied pertly, "Iskander!" Whenever the Moors see anything marvellous or ancient, they ascribe it to Alexander the Great, to Pharaoh, to Solomon, or even to Nimrod, as caprice leads them, believing that these three or four personages created all the wondrous and monstrous things in the world. But we have an instance here, how soon through ignorance, or the want of records, a modern thing may become ancient in the minds of the vulgar. This fort was built after Mogador, which town is not yet a century old.

racter of the Moor, he can sometimes indulge himself in pleasantry and caricature. The Moors have made caricatures of the three last emperors, assisted by some Spanish renegade artist: these Princes are Yezid, Suleiman, and Abd Errahman. Yezid is represented as throwing away money with one hand, and cutting off heads with the other, depicting his ferocity in destroying his enemies, and his generosity in heaping favours on his friends. Suleiman is represented as reading the Koran, in the character of a devout and good man. The present Sultan is hit off capitally, with one hand holding a bag of money behind him, and with the other stretched out before him, begging for more.

H B could not have better caricatured the three Shereefian Sultans. The Moors affirmed that Muley Abd Errahman will keep faith with no one where his avarice is concerned, and, when he can, he will sell a monopoly twice or thrice, receiving money from each party. Of his meanness and avarice, I adduce two anecdotes. Four years ago, Muley Abd Errahman ordered some blond for his Harem from Mr. Willshire. Just when I was leaving Mogador, his Imperial Highness graciously returned it to our merchant with the message—" It's too dear." Not long before, a man was murdered upon the neutral land of two adjacent provinces, and a thousand dollars were taken from his baggage. In such cases, the Governor of the district is mulcted both for the murder and robbery. The Emperor claimed two thousand dollars from one of the provinces, for the father of the murdered man. This province escaped upon the plea that the murder had not been committed within its territory. The other province refused to satisfy the demand for the same reason. His Imperial Highness then made both provinces pay 2,000 dollars each, keeping one two thousand for himself, for the trouble he had of enforcing payment.

The people of Sous not long ago had a quarrel, which the Emperor fomented. Its

Sheikhs fought; his Imperial Highness sent troops to turn the balance of the fray, and to pacify the country. Then, he made the belligerents pay each 40,000 dollars, as pacification-money, the value of which he levied on slaves. In this politic way, the Imperial miser replenishes his coffers, and "eats up" his loving subjects.

I made the acquaintance of Mr. Treppass, the Austrian consul, and Chancellor of the French consulate. Mr. Treppass has been upwards of twenty years in this country, and was himself once an Imperial merchant, but sold his business, preferring a small stipend and his liberty, to being a vassal of the Emperor, fed in luxury and lodged in a fine house. We had a long conversation upon the various topics connected with this country.

Mr. Treppass says, the present system of the court is resistance to all innovation, to all strangers. But the pressure of the French on the Algerine frontier is agitating the internal state of this country. Money, which in other countries goes a long way, will almost do every thing with the Government of Morocco. It will also effect much with the people. Some fifty years ago, a Geneose merchant, resident in Mogador, had the two provinces of Hhaha and Shedma under his control, and could have made himself Sultan over them; this he effected solely by the distribution of money. The Sultan of the time was in open war with a pretender; his Imperial Highness begged for the assistance of the all-powerful merchant. The merchant bought the affections and allegiance of the people, and firmly established the Sultan on his throne.

The influence of the merchont was now prodigious, and the Sultan himself became alarmed. Not being able to rest, and being in hourly dread of the Genoese, the Sultan ordered his officers to seize the merchant secretly, and put him on board a vessel then weighing anchor for Europe. When the merchant was placed on board, this message was delivered to him—" Our Sultan is extremely obliged to you, sir, for the great services you rendered him, by establishing him on his throne! but our Sultan says, 'If you could place him on the throne, you could also pull him off again.' Therefore you must leave our country. Our Sultan graciously gives you a portion of your wealth to carry away with you!" The officers then shipped several chests of money, jewels, and other valuables to be placed to the account of the merchant, and the Sultan-making Genoese quitted Morocco for ever.

The Moors reported to me that the French were building some factories, with a fort, upon some unclaimed land along the coast, equi-distant between Aghadir and Wadnoun. It is probably near Fort Hillsboro of the maps, and which Mr. Davidson calls Isgueder. A Moor was accused by the authorities of Mogador of being mixed up with the transaction, and immediately sent to the south, where he has not been heard of since. Another report is, that the French are only building a factory. The spot of land has near it a small port and a good spring of water; quantities of bricks and lime have been deposited there; French vessels of war from the Senegal have been coasting and surveying up and down, touching at the place.

The new port is called Yedoueesai. I inquired particularly respecting this project; but Mr. Treppass stated positively, that the French had wholly abandoned the idea of establishing commercial relations with the Sheikh of Wadnoun, or any tribes thereabouts, whatever might have been their original intentions. Vessels of war have frequently visited the coast of Wadnoun, finding it the worst in all Africa. They, however, now maintain friendly relations with the Sheikh, in the event of shipwrecks or other disasters, happening to French vessels.

Nevertheless, it was at the particular request

of the French Consul of Mogador, that his Government broke off all communications with the Sheikh, the Emperor having repeatedly complained to the Consul against this intercourse assuming a commercial or diplomatic character.* The whole coast, from the port of Mogador to the river Senegal, has been, within the last few years, surveyed by the French vessels of war, particularly by Captain E. Bouet; and there is sufficient evidence in the reports of the people, and the remonstrances of the Maroquine Government, to prove that the French did attempt a settlement on the part of the coast above stated, but that it failed.

The French took the idea of the undertaking from Davidson, who proposed to Lord Palmerston to enter into communication with the

---

* Certainly, to establish relations with the Southern provinces of Morocco, that is, Sous and Wadnoun, would greatly injure the trade of Mogador, and, therefore, the Consuls, as well as the Moorish Authorities, set their faces against any direct intercourse being opened with the South.

Sheikh of Wadnoun, and establish a factory on the coast, somewhere about the river Noun, just below Cape Noun. A British vessel of war was sent down with presents for the Sheikh, and to ascertain the whereabout of the fine harbour reported to exist there by the Sheikh and his people. This attempt of our government was as fruitless as that of the French afterwards. Indeed, at the very time an English brig of war was searching about for this port, and seeking an interview with the Sheikh of Wadnoun on the coast, Davidson was murdered on the southern frontier just as he was penetrating the Sahara.

It is not improbable, however, that the knowledge of this recommendation of Davidson, which, from the Sheikh's people themselves, would naturally reach the court of Morocco, might have excited that jealous court to compass in some way his death, or at any rate thwart his expedition to Timbuctoo, for the Emperor is exceedingly jealous of any European holding communication with the south. The Sheikh

Barook is, in spite of all this, very anxious to begin an intercourse with Europeans; and not long ago, a messenger arrived with a bag of money for the Jew, Cohen, telling him to take some out of it, and to go to the Sheikh who wished to see him. But Cohen would not expose himself to the displeasure of the Emperor, although he has English protection.

Wadnoun is a quasi-independent Sheikhdom of the empire. The Sheikh of Wadnoun pays no tithes nor other imposts, and only sends an annual present as a mark of vassal-homage to the Emperor. Sous, which adjoins this province, is more immediately under the power of the Sultan of the Shereefs, but the tithes are not so easily collected in the south as in the north. Much depends on the ability of the governor, who rules the whole of the district in the name of the Emperor. The imperial authority is maintained principally by prompting disunion amongst the Sheikhs; Sous being divided into numerous districts, each district having an independent Sheikh.

By confusion and divisions among themselves, the Emperor rules all as paramount-lord. When will people learn to be united, so that by union they may win their freedom and independence? Alas! never. Wadnoun is treated, however, very tenderly; for if the Emperor were to attempt the subjugation of this country, the malcontents of Sous would join the Sheikh, and his authority would probably be overthrown in all the south.

Sous is the richest of these provinces, and equal to any other of the northern districts. Its trade in dates, ostrich feathers, wax, wool, and hides, particularly in gums, almonds, and slaves, is very great. All the Saharan caravans must pass through this country, except those proceeding *viâ* Tafilett to Fez. Teroudant, its capital, is a very ancient city, and was built by the ancient Berbers. It has a circumference of walls capable of containing eighty thousand people, but the actual population does not exceed twenty thousand. Its inhabitants are very industrious, and the Moors excel in the art of dyeing.

Noun, or Wadnoun, as this country and its capital are sometimes called, Mr. Davidson briefly describes as a large district, having many clusters of inhabitants. The town where the Sheikh resides, is of good size, and has a millah, or Jew's quarter, besides a good market. It stands on the river (such as it is) distant twenty two miles from the sea.

The river Noun rises in the mountains above Souk Aisa or Assa, and is there called Wad-el-Aisa; and, passing through the district of Wadnoun, it takes the name of Assaka. The ancient name of this river was Daradus. The territory around is not very fertile on account of the neighbourhood of the Desert, but produces gum, wax, and ostrich feathers in abundance. The inhabitants are mostly Arabs with a sprinkling of Shelouh, estimated by

Gräberg* at 2,000. The population is somewhat thickly scattered; there are at least twenty villages between the district of Stuka and Wadnoun.

The annexed is a sketch of Wadnoun after the design left by Mr. Davidson.

* Gräberg says *Noun* means the "river of eels," Davidson derives the name from a Portuguese queen called Nounah; but his editor says the name is properly Nul, was so written when the Arabs possessed Portugal, and that Queen Nunah is a modern invention.

Wadnoun is an important rendezvous of caravans. Many Timbuctoo caravans break up here, and some Saharan. Several Saharan merchants come no further north, disposing of their slaves and goods to Maroquine merchants, who meet them in this place.

It is safe travelling through these countries, provided no extraordinary plot be laid for taking away a traveller's life, as in the case of European explorers attempting to penetrate the interior. Mr. Treppass thinks that, notwithstanding the ill-will of the Moorish Government, Davidson could have succeeded in his attempted journey to Timbuctoo had he been more circumspect. He gave out to all persons whom he met that he was going to Timbuctoo. This insured his being stopped and murdered *en route* by some party or other, more especially as he at last abandoned the idea of protecting himself by a caravan-party, and started alone. But I am not altogether of this opinion. Too much publicity is certainly injurious to a journey of discovery, and far and near awakens attention and suspicion; but a too sudden and unexpected appearance in the towns of the Desert, equally excites distrust and suspicion, if not hostile feelings.

Mr. Robertson, whilst at Morocco, heard one of the numerous versions of the death of Mr. Davidson. He is said to have been killed by the mere freak of a young Arab, who wished to have the pleasure of killing a Christian, and who called out to his companions, " Come, let us go and have a shot at the Christian." The party of Arabs to whom this mischievous young man belonged, was afterwards extremely grieved at what had been done. One of the Arabs, in plundering the baggage, lost his hand by breaking a bottle containing aqua fortis. The glass cut a large gash, and the aqua fortis entering immediately, consumed the hand. The people cried out, " The devils of the Christian are in the water!" From all I have heard, the great fault of Davidson appears to have been his wish ing to travel as like " a fine gentleman." This prejudiced all his travelling-companions against him, and could not fail to render him unpopular wherever he went.

It is of no use for a man to cry out in the Desert, "I am an Englishman!" he must exclaim, "I am an Arab, and will do and suffer like an Arab." If any one were to ask me, "What would carry a man to Timbuctoo through the Desert? is it courage, or money, or prudence?" I would reply, "The first thing is suffering, the second is suffering, and the last is suffering."* I consulted an old man

---

* Whatever may have been Mr. Davidson's faults, I scarcely doubt that the first impressions of Mr. Consul-General Hay were correct. He says, "I *fear, however,* that *I am not to expect much assistance* from him," (Mr. Hay); and hints, in other parts of his Journal, that Mr. Hay was rather disposed to throw difficulties in his way, than to render him efficient aid. Mr. Hay's son (which is very natural) attempts to exculpate his father in an appendix to his "Western Barbary," and some will, perhaps, think he has done so successfully. My experience of the diplomatic skill of the late Consul, does not permit me to coincide with this favourable

on this journey to Timbuctoo. He could not undertake a voyage being too old. He mentioned names of places *en route*, and said they travelled by the stars, which star-travelling is all stuff. He recommended going by sea as much nearer. Very little satisfactory information can be obtained from Maroquine Moors, who would rather mislead than direct you.

I endeavoured to open a correspondence with the South on the Anti-Slavery question. At first, I thought of going to Wadnoun on receiving an invitation from the Sheikh, but when I proposed this to Mr. Willshire, he insisted on my relinquishing such a project, inasmuch as having placed myself at the direction of the Consul-General, as recommended by the Earl of Aberdeen, I was not at liberty to differ from opinion. The greater probability is, that if Mr. Davidson had been left to his own "inspirations," and allowed complete liberty of action, he would have succeeded in reaching Timbuctoo; but his health does not appear to have been sufficiently robust, or himself acclimated, to have brought him back from his perilous adventure.

the advice, which Mr. Hay and himself might tender me. I saw there was some reason in this, and submitted though with great reluctance. However, I wrote two letters to Sheikh Barook of Wadnoun, stating the views and objects of the Anti-Slavery Society.

I had some difficulty in finding a courier, who would undertake the delicate mission of conveying the letters. But Mr. Treppass and the French Consul, M. Jorelle, felt themselves more at liberty in the matter than our Consul, and determined to assist me, M. Jorelle very justly observing, " We will sow the seeds of liberty, if we can do nothing more." Indeed, I am greatly obliged to that gentleman for the interest he took in my mission, and the assistance he rendered me on this and other occasions. After my return to England, I received two letters from the Sheikh in answer to those I had written to him. The Sheikh, afraid lest his letter might fall into the hands of Government, after many compliments, begs me to get the

Emperor first to move in the question, adding, "what he makes free, we will make free;" for he says in another place, "We act as he acts, according to the *treek* (ordinance) of God and his Prophet."

Sheikh Barook also protests that he has but little power in these matters, living as he does in the Desert. As I did not seek for any thing beyond an answer to my letters, and was only anxious that he should know the sentiments of the Anti-Slavery Society, I was not all disappointed. I knew too much of the pro-slavery feeling once existing in a strong party in England, and the mighty struggles which we had passed through to obtain British Abolition, to expect anything more than a respectful answer to anti-slavery letters from a Prince of the Desert, whose revenues were raised chiefly from the duties levied upon slave-caravans passing through his territory. I only attempted to scatter the seeds of liberty over the slave-tracks of the Desert, leaving the budding forth and the growth to the irrigating influences of that merciful and wise God, who has made all men of one flesh and blood.

I visited the families of Jewish merchants during the Passover, in company with Mr. and Mrs. Elton. Christians here visit the Jews twice a year, at the feast of the Passover and Tabernacles. In return, Jews visit Christians on New Year's day. This laudable practice promotes social harmony between the Jews and Christians.

In the house of one of our Jewish friends (Mr. Levi's) I assisted at the celebration of the evening of the Passover. There is nothing very particular in this ceremony, except a great deal of reading. The drinking of the four cups* of wine, and the eating of the bitter herbs, emblems of the joys and the sorrows attending the

---

* These cups hold at least a pint each, and every adult male is expected to empty four, if not six. Of course, they get beastly intoxicated, and suffer a day or two of illness afterwards, a very just punishment.

deliverance from Egyptian bondage, are the more difficult parts of the ceremony. The children naturally feel most the disagreeableness of eating the bitter herbs, and several times, as soon as they put them into their mouths, they spat them out again under the table. The drinking of an excessive quantity of wine, is also attended with not a little inconvenience, and one would think Bacchus was the deity worshipped, and not the God of the Jews and Christians. When will mankind learn that violation of the physical economy of their nature can never be acceptable to the Great Creator?

I do not say that European Israelites indulge so much in these excesses as Barbary Jews, but I imagine that the germ of the debauch is found in the Talmudical religion of both classes. But, since I should be very sorry were a Jew to hold up to me the mummeries of Popery or of the Greek Church, as the mirror of my own religion, I am not disposed to animadvert upon the generally decorous worship of European Israelites.

It requires three full days to get through this business of visiting. In truth, it is a very serious affair, for we were obliged to eat cake, and sip sherbet, or white brandy, at every house we went to, otherwise we should confer an affront upon our friends. At all times, a great quantity of white brandy, which the Jews distil themselves, is drunk, but especially on these occasions.

The Governor of Mogador gave orders, not long ago, that no Mussulman should enter the Jewish quarter, to prevent the faithful from being seduced into drinking this insidious spirit. I shall just mention what a Christian is obliged to conform to, whilst visiting the Barbary Jews on these high days and holidays.

1st. You must eat a piece of cake, at least of *one* sort, if not of several kinds, and drink a little brandy, wine somets, or boiled juice of the grape, or sherbet. In many of the houses, they give nothing but brandy, which is tastefully placed out on small round tables, as at a pastry-cook's shop.

2nd. You must admire the new dresses of the ladies, who are radiantly and sumptuously attired " in flaming purple and refulgent gold," their ornaments likewise of gold, silver, and all manner of precious stones ; for the daughters of Israel are, as on bridal days, all begemmed, bejewelled, and diamonded, stuck over with gems as thick as stars " seen in the galaxy or milky-way." On these festivals, it is absolutely a matter of orthodox observance that the Jews and Jewesses should wear something new. Some have entirely new dresses.

3rd. Any thing new or remarkable in the house, or household furniture, must be noticed or admired

4th. You must carry with you in your memorandum-book, or at the tip of your tongue, a good assortment of first-rate compliments of the season.

If these are spiced with a little scandal of your neighbours, or the party you have just left, so much the better; they are more relished.

Now you are obliged to visit twenty or thirty families per diem; and you are literally passing through doors, square-courts, and corridors, crossing patios and quadrangles, walking up and down stairs, getting up and sitting down from morning to night, during these three mortal days. It will be seen then, that these Passover and Tabernacle visits are tremendous affairs, and require Herculean strength to get through their polite duties. They may be days of jovial festivity to Jews, but certainly they are days of labour and annoyance to Gentiles.

But I must now give an account of one or two remarkable personages whom we visited. The first was Madame Bousac, a Jewess of this country. Her father was a grandee at

Court in the days of former emperors, and the greatest merchant of his time, and she represented as an aristocrat among her people, a modern Esther, standing and pleading between the Sultan and her nation. This lady is the only native woman in the country, Mooress or Jewess, who has tact or courage enough to go and speak to the Emperor, and state her request with an unfaltering voice beneath the awful shadow of the Shereefian presence! Madame Bousac accompanied the merchants to Morocco, to pay her respects to the Emperor. Among other modest or confidential demands which the lady made on the Imperial benevolence, was that of an advance to her husband of ten thousand dollars. His Imperial Highness was immediately obliged to give a formal assent before his court.

She then visited the Harem, and felt herself quite at home. All the ladies, wives or concubines of the Emperor, waited upon her; and served her with tea and bread and butter.

The presentation of bread and butter and cups of tea, is said to be the highest honour conferred on visitors, but why or wherefore I have not heard.

Madame Bousac gave us some account of the Morocco harem, which we may suppose is like that of Fez and Miknas. The number of these ladies was some two hundred. They are all attired alike, except the four wives, who dress a little more in the style of Sultanas. I am sorry to be obliged to disabuse the reader of the romance and oriental colouring attached to our ideas of the harem, by giving Madame Bousac's simile of these angelic houries. This lady said, "they are like a string of charity-school girls going to church on a Sunday morning."

Their penurious lord keeps down their pin-money to the lowest point, and is not more liberal to his ladies than to his other subjects. Former sultans were accustomed to allow their ladies half a dollar a day, but these have but twopence, or at least fourpence. Muley Abd Errahman even traffics in his beauties, and will now and then make a present of one to a governor, in consideration of receiving an adequate return of money, or presents. Sometimes, the Moors pay their Shereefian Sultan a similar compliment, by presenting him with slaves from their harem.*

Madame Bousac is, of course, a perfect lady according to Moorish ideas, but her fascinations on the mind of the Emperor, arise more from her wit and ability than her feminine grace and

---

* But I do not think it reaches the point of complaisance, noticed by Monsieur Chénier, when he was French Consul in 1767. He says, "The veneration of the Moors is so great for this Prince, that they deem themselves happy whenever one of their daughters is admitted to share his couch." On the other hand, many of the beauties presented by the Sultan to his ministers, although brought out of his harems, are virgins. The poor ladies in the royal harems are only so much stock, from which their Lord and tyrant picks and chooses.

delicacy. She is anything but a beauty, according to our ideas, being of a dark complexion, of middle height, of large and powerful muscular proportions, very upright, as if bending backwards, and with a hoarse and masculine voice. Like most women in this part of the world, she is married to a man old enough to be her father, or even grandfather, being even more than double her age.

She herself may be about thirty, at which age the beauty of Barbary women is gone for ever. Such is the court-dame who has courage enough to speak to the Emperor of Morocco in public. She conversed with us about her affairs, telling us the Emperor had not yet advanced to her husband the loan of 10,000 dollars as promised, nor did she expect it, for she knew his avarice. "Rather would he sell one of his Sultanas." But he had sent her a present of four haiks, which she shewed us; they were extremely fine and white. "These," she observed, " are the ten thousand dollars paid in private, but which the Sultan could not refuse me in public."

Another character whom we visited, was the distinguished Rabbi, Coriante. The priest entertained us with dissertations upon various subjects. First of slavery. "It is unlawful to steal blacks, the Mosaic law denouncing such theft with the punishment of death. Nevertheless, if the Jews of this country had the power, they would enslave the Mussulmen, and well castigate them."

This latter remark, Coriante uttered with an emphasis, denoting the revenge which his countrymen would inflict upon their Mahometan oppressors, who had kept them in chains for a series of ages. He remarked, however, that the Sultan might give way on the question of negro slavery, after the first shock to his prejudices.

The Rabbi treated us with wine, but one of us, moved by curiosity, having touched the bottle, he remarked to his daughter in an under-tone; "It's all gone," (the rest of the wine is spoiled). Among these extremely superstitious Barbary rabbies, it is a pollution to their wine if a Christian touch even the bottle containing the juice of the grape, and they will not drink it afterwards.

We asked the reason of his not being able to drink, and found it was, first, because women work in the vineyards, and the second, because the Pope pronounces his blessing upon the vintage. After these Jews have eaten meat, they are obliged to wait some time before they can eat butter, or drink milk; in fact, their superstitions are numberless. The Rabbi read to us portions of the proverbs of Solomon, and told us Solomon was well acquainted with steam-engines and railways, "Only they were of no use in the Holy Land when God was always with his people." He then gave us his blessing, and me this solemn warning. "Take care the Emperor does not cut of your head, as he has cut off the head of our young Darmon."*

* Friend Phillips is always wrestling with these prejudices of Barbary Jews. When his wife was delivered of a daughter, he was determined to have as much "fuss" made of the child as if it had been a son, to spite the prejudices of his brethren. So, when he went out for a walk with his wife, he would walk always arm-in-arm with her, although she was a Jewess of this country, which caused great annoyance to his woman-oppressing brethren.

END OF VOL. I.

LONDON:
Printed by A. Schulze, 13, Poland Street.

www.ingramcontent.com/pod-product-compliance
Lightning Source LLC
Chambersburg PA
CBHW060414170426
43199CB00013B/2130